Darbar
Arts Culture
Heritage

Ajay Joglekar Ajoy Chakrabarty Amrit P
Anutosh Degharia Arjun Kumar Arvind Pa
Dagar Bhai Baldeep Singh Bhupinder Sing
Carl Herring Chandra Chakrabarty Deb
Dharambir Singh Dharmesh Parmer Dr
Modarelli Gunwant Kaur Gurdain Rayatt G
Rayatt Harmeet Virdee Hary Kumar Siv
Jesse Bannister Kala Ramnath Kaushi
Zuckerman Kiranpal Singh Kumar Bose M
Mysore Manjunath Nayan Ghosh Neyveli
Sartha Mukherjee Parveen Sultana Pete
Mallick Purbayan Chatterjee R N Prakash
Mishra Ranjana Ghatak Ravi Shankar U
Mistry Ronu Majumdar Rupinder Kaur
Subramanyan Sanju Sahai Shabaz Hussa
Soumik Datta Subhankar Banerjee Sukhde
Channa Surmeet Dhadyalla Swapan Ch
Uday Bhawalkar Upneet Dhadyalla Vishwa M

siya Anindo Chatterjee Anurekha Ghosh
ikh Ashwini Bhide Deshpande Bahauddin
Chaggar Bickram Ghosh Binderjeet Neer
riya Das Debojyoti Bose Dharam Varia
yotsna Srikanth Edurado Niebla Giuliano
rprit Matharu Harjinderpal Singh Harkirat
Hiren Chate Irshad Khan Javier Geras
i Chakraborty Kaviraj Dhadyalla Ken
njit Rasiya Mounir Baziz Mysore Chandan
enkatesh Nina Virdee Pandit Jasraj Partha
Lockett Prashant Mallick Prem Kumar
Rajvir Cheema Rakesh Chaurasia Ramesh
adhay Rehmat Rayatt Rimpa Siva Rohit
S Varadharajan Sandeep Mishra Sanjay
Shahid Parvez Shashwati Mandal Paul
p Dhanjal Sukhwinder Singh Surdarshan
dhuri Tarun Jasani Tejendra Majumdar
han Bhatt Viswanth Shridkar Yogesh Samsi

darbar
SOUTH ASIAN MUSIC FESTIVAL

In loving memory of
Bhai Gurmit Singh Ji Virdee
(1937-2005)

Presented by: tablaonline   SAMSC   peepul

Sponsored by: bmi   ARTS COUNCIL   Heritage Lottery Fund

Darbar
Arts Culture
Heritage

Published and distributed by
Darbar Arts Culture Heritage Trust

Darbar
Arts Culture Heritage Trust
264-266 Leicester Road
Wigston, Leicester
LE18 1HQ
United Kingdom

Phone: +44 (0) 1162 987 387
Fax: +44 (0) 1162 987 487
Email: info@darbar.org.uk
Web: www.darbar.org.uk

Edited and Produced by **Darbar**
Book design by **Parent**

Distribution Support
www.grangehotels.com

Cover Image:
Pandit Kumar Bose
Performing a Tabla Solo in
Teental–5th March 2006

ISBN 978-0-9561697-0-9
Printed by **Team Impression**
www.team-impression.com

Preface

Darbar | Arts Culture Heritage has been a labour of love to keep alive the classical music heritage of the Indian sub-continent.

Beginning life as the Darbar South Asian Music Festival in 2006, the event - the largest annual gathering of Indian classical musicians outside of the sub-continent - quickly became a catalyst for change. The first Festival was a tribute to Bhai Gurmit Singh Virdee, a talented tabla player, inspirational teacher, and a spiritual person who made a selfless contribution to Britain's music scene.

This book - which brings together writing from musicians, journalists, music students, museum curators, and promoters - provides a snapshot of the state of this musical genre in the early twenty-first century. The book, together with Darbar's work on the ground, is aimed to make Indian classical music more accessible to the modern audience.

Written by people who live and work in Britain, it portrays the changing face of Indian Classical Music. It addresses issues of heritage and culture, and how the music could be kept alive in a fast-changing world of information overload, and competing forms of arts and entertainment.

The first Festival was a tribute to Bhai Gurmit Singh Virdee, a talented tabla player, inspirational teacher, and a spiritual person who made a selfless contribution to Britain's music scene.

Each piece, from the personal journeys by Dr Ranjeev Singh Bhangoo, Gurdain Singh Rayatt and Soumik Datta; the overview by Simon Broughton; the state of music training by John Ball and a glimpse into the technological musical future by Dharambir Singh highlights a small piece of the bigger picture. The selection of the writers is designed to show that young people are deeply interested in this art form. And, ultimately, it is young musicians who are going to keep the music live and relevant to the modern audiences.

Darbar prides itself in the quality of its imagery and we hope that the photographs – which are without parallel in this musical genre – do justice to the beauty of the art form.

This book, like any worthwhile venture, would not be possible without the hard work of many people. I would like to thank all the writers who have given time to write the words in this book; Arnhel de Serra for his wonderful reportage photography and Jonathan Worth for the portrait photography; SkyArts for producing the DVD; Parent Design for the new branding of Darbar, designing the book and pulling the material together. Thank you to Team Impression for creating such a beautifully bound book. We would also like to thank the Heritage Lottery Fund for providing the funds to publish this book and the Arts Council of England, East Midlands for supporting Darbar.

The Darbar team is indebted to Bhai Sahib Mohinder Singh Ji, spiritual successor of Guru Nanak Nishkam Sewak Jatha who stood by and gave his blessings to Darbar and its work from its inception.

A special thanks is made to all the members of the Virdee family, and especially Mrs Mohinder Kaur Virdee who provided nourishment, good humour and motherly advice to Sandeep and I as we worked away into the small hours.

Lastly, I would like to thank my wife, Manjit, who gave support and guidance throughout, and my children, Mandip and Aaron whose daddy, who should have been playing with them, was often found staring at the computer screen to meet yet another self-imposed deadline.

We hope you enjoy the book as much as we have enjoyed creating it.

Kulbir S Natt,
Director, Darbar

About the Contributors

John Ball

is a talented instrumentalist who plays both santoor and tabla. He is committed to the promotion of Indian classical music through regular teaching, performances in schools and local communities and writing.

Dr Ranjeev Singh Bhangoo

is a consultant neurosurgeon at King's College Hospital with a special interest in brain tumours and paediatric neurosurgery. He is an unaccomplished musician who never got beyond the recorder! Nevertheless, he has had a lifelong interest in the arts and particularly music, literature and visual arts.

Simon Broughton

is a writer, film maker and editor of the world music magazine, Songlines. TV documentaries for the BBC and Channel 4 include 'Breaking the Silence: Music in Afghanistan', 'Sufi Soul: The Mystic Music of Islam' and 'Mariza and the Story of Fado.'

James Burkmar

has worked as a musician, a promoter, music leader and facilitator in prison settings and a music officer in the Arts Council England. Currently, he is working as a consultant with "brilliant people, projects and partners around the country on music and wider creative industries projects'.

Soumik Datta

is a UK-based classically trained sarod player and a member of the group, Samay. He is a product of both his Indian roots and his western upbringing. He has also experimented with jazz, blues and flamenco styles.

Rolf Killius

is a member of the Kala Collective (www.kalacollective.com). It works with people to create projects that introduce South Asian arts to new audiences, create fresh opportunities for artists and connect communities and cultures across the globe. He is a consultant for museums, exhibitions and media as well as an ethnomusicologist, sound recordist, and radio journalist.

Gurdain Singh Rayatt

is one of the UK's brightest young tabla players. Currently, he is combining his degree course in English and Film at King's College, London as well as continuing to improve his tabla from Pandit Shankar Ghosh. Gurdain has played at several prestigious festivals including Saptak and Harballabh in India.

Derek Roberts

is a sound engineer at Indian classical music record label Sense World Music. He is a musician and has experience of live event management, theatre, sound design, studio and live production and location video recording.

Jameela Siddiqi

is a novelist, journalist and broadcaster who came to Britain as a refugee from Uganda in 1972. She won a Sony Gold award for her series 'Songs of the Sufi Mystics' on BBC World Service Radio (1997) and was presenter of the acclaimed Radio 3 series 'Nights of the Goddess' (2000). She has written extensively on Indian classical music. Her novels include 'The Feast of the Nine Virgins' and 'Bombay Gardens'.

Dharambir Singh Dhadyalla

is a leading sitar player in the UK and Indian Classical Music musicologist. He is a NESTA fellow; a lecturer in Indian Music at Leeds University; set up SAA-UK 1997, a leading South Asian Arts organisation. He specialises in Indian Music training and has an FTLC qualification from Trinity College. He's working on an Indian music accreditation programme and is an Advisor on an Indian Music degree at Bharti Vidya Bhavan, London.

Sandeep Singh Virdee

is Darbar's Artistic Director. He taught tabla alongside his late father, one of the most respected teachers in the UK. He was also involved in 'TAAL Rhythms of India', the leading tabla promoter in the UK, who put on concerts, "In Conversation" sessions with artists, and workshops. Sandeep is also an experienced photographer and video cameraman.

Bhai Gurmit Singh Virdee
Giving his blessings at the launch of
Tablaonline (the precursor to Darbar)
at Symphony Hall, Birmingham, 2nd May 2004
Photo by Gurwinder Singh Soor

01
Darbar
Arts Culture
Heritage

Author Sandeep Singh Virdee

Sandeep Singh Virdee
Author

Indian classical music has been on the British arts scene for more than two generations. Since the 1950s when the legendary Ustad Ali Akbar Khan Indian and Pandit Chatur Lal gave the first major Indian classical concert in Britain, dozens of south asian arts organisations have spawned; music classes have flourished up; record labels have released hundreds of performances, and partnerships with established institutions have taken the music to a wider audience. It was in this mix that the Darbar Festival arrived on the scene in 2006. And while we continue to develop and add innovations to the event, in the run up to each festival we sometimes ask ourselves why do we spend our time, energy and, indeed, money on it? Looking after some 40 artists, keeping them and the audience happy and making sure everything runs smoothly is no small task and during yet another sleep-deprived working day, this question is difficult to answer. What follows is an attempt to address some of the issues behind this question. It is also a tribute to our parents' generation whose enterprise, adventurism and dedication to create a better life for themselves, and us, through education and hard work has allowed an organisation such as Darbar to flourish.

But first some context. Many of our generation may not remember the exact words of Enoch Powell's 'rivers of blood' speech but its consequences indelibly shape our less than sepia-tinted memories. Many of our parents were born in the last years of the Raj or as subjects in colonies like those in British East Africa grew up in a generation fluent in their mother tongue, ancestral lore and an affection for the English language. They fiercely believed education was the way to beat the system and overcome prejudice. They understood that though Britain needed them they weren't really welcome, and that goodwill, like the friends, wealth and assets so many had to leave behind, was not transferable from colony to mother country.

Many a parent sacrificed their aspirations, including leisure and cultural pursuits, to give their children a chance at a better life. In return, they expected more of their children: the mantra our generation grew up with was not just 'Hari Om', 'WaheGuru' or 'Inshallah' but rather 'you have to be better than the rest to get the same opportunities'. Complaining about the system's unfairness was not an option.

For most arts and music played a small part. For many it was relegated to a Sunday morning programme on BBC Television called 'Nai Zindagi Nai Jeevan' ('New Life, New Beginning') where the presenters looked like fossils from before the flood. The programme did not live up to the title, nor spoke to our generation. Our parents felt that getting their children to watch, what many considered an ordeal, would help to keep us in touch with our roots. Occasionally, though, the agony was worth it, when at the end of the programme there was a short piece of classical music or dance that hinted that there was more to being an Indian immigrant than getting good grades at school. In some young minds a hint of a fuller less colonially derived identity began to form.

But most of the time our parents were too busy trying to get ahead in life and most had little time for the arts. Meanwhile, at school we were all 'Pakis'. Many felt we were getting enough flak, so it was hardly worth the trouble to emphasise our differences even more by asserting our cultural identity. Many young south Asians were often turned off by their own culture. And this was sometimes not helped by many migrants who arrived directly from the sub-continent who maintained a culture that was fossilised in the late 1950s and early 1960s. The culture had cut itself off from the original plant in India, which, particularly in its urban form, continued to evolve, diversify and flourish. In Britain, the offshoot clung to a remembered past with a stubbornness that left the second

For most people arts and music was relegated to a Sunday morning programme on BBC Television called 'Nai Zindagi Nai Jeevan' ('New Life, New Beginning') where the presenters looked like fossils from before the flood. **Sandeep Singh Virdee**

generation with roots in two seed beds, neither of which seemed particularly attractive in firmly planting down our roots.

It was Southall that first bucked the trend in the 1970s with the production of home-grown Bhangra music. The singers, the product of a large, openly self-confident Punjabi community, spoke to and for our generation. From Channi singing with Alaap at a cousin's wedding to John Peel playing a Bhangra track on radio, the effect on a community's self-confidence, sense of worth and sense of belonging cannot be overemphasised. Songs like 'Apna Sangeet' symbolised music that spoke to the second generation. The first title 'Our Music' spoke on so many different levels, OUR music, OUR language, OUR culture and OUR community and by this it meant not the culture of the Punjab, but the culture of British Punjabis - we began to look forward and not back.

Whilst many were forging a new identity through music, others (and often the same individuals), were rediscovering their heritage in a piecemeal and haphazard manner, like finding a record in an Indian record store or your family. Many, like myself, turned towards India's classical music. This discovery may have in part been due to a confidence and luxury of time stemming from the security provided by our parents' generation and reinforced by a sense of pride in our ancestors. Their classical musical forms were marked by tolerance, innovation, academic rigour, restraint and professionalism. They were inspired by the myriad religious traditions, and the theoretical underpinnings of the music were a demonstration that the Indian tradition was not just one that shunned analysis and science in favour of emotion.

Recorded music was followed by live concerts: Ustad Vilyat Khan (the greatest sitar player of the 20th century) at London's Royal Festival Hall to lesser-known musicians at smaller venues. But many concerts soon started to fade in memory, as it became evident that the potential that was hinted at in the recordings did not begin to materialise, despite the lack of constraint of time. Many conversations with artists and organisers later, it emerged that both believed that the diaspora and western audiences wanted 'classical light'. They believed that British audiences did not have the background, training and the cultured appetite to appreciate

and digest classical music at its most refined and raw. Instead, performances were generally full of musical gymnastics, pyrotechnics and technical proficiency. These, and not artistic insight, were seen as the benchmarks of excellence. To summarise, the assumed demographic was seen as 'Classic FM' and not 'BBC Radio 3'.

So we began to set up our own concerts where we invited artists we wanted to listen to. We asked them to push themselves, their musical form and their audience to the limit. Most of these initial concerts were tabla solo concerts. Our choice reflected our own liking for classical Indian percussion and because it is particularly popular amongst us young Sikhs as it is a vital element of Sikh religious worship. Many artists, who initially balked at the idea of performing 2 to 3 hour classical percussion solos for our audiences left with a sense of awe after performing in front of teenage cognoscenti.

Darbar, which was born as a tribute Festival in 2006, tries to live up to these musical underpinnings, but it ventures into the full gamut of Indian classical music. We aim to expose the audience to a full range of classical artists representing the full range of traditions including instrumental, dhrupad, khayal, carnatic and thumri. The audience, itself, no longer the wealthy elite but everyday folk from all walks of life. The artist is no longer bound by the tyranny of a powerful patron but is free to experiment, educate and push themselves artistically. They do this in the presence of fellow artists who are sitting in the audience. The artist, on stage, knows that they cannot get away with anything less than his or her best. This mingling of artists, unique to Darbar, recreates an important aspect of the

Bhai Sahib Mohinder Singh Ji Lighting of Jot (spiritual candle)
Marking the the launch of the Darbar Festival / 3rd March 2006

Pandit Anindo Chatterjee, Pandit Swapan Chaudhuri & Pandit Kumar Bose
Three tabla legends on same stage

Pandit Anindo Chatterjee [ajrara gharana]
Solo in Teental / 3rd March 2006

Pandit Swapan Chaudhuri [lucknow gharana]
Solo in Teental / 5th March 2006

Pandit Kumar Bose [benares gharana]
Solo in Teental / 4th March 2006

old courtly tradition where a coterie of artists living and playing in close proximity for a few days creates new enthusiasms and creativity. This aspect of the courtly tradition is further recapitulated in the Shivir, where UK musicians of exceptional ability and dedication are hot-housed for a week with leading Indian musicians prior to the main festival. The Shivir, part of Darbar's artist development programme, is a specific response to the need to maintain the Guru-shishya (pupil) tradition in a modern Britain.

Darbar is not only an expression of our love of a shared heritage but it also represents our dreams for the future. As such, a number of the artists chosen for each festival while representing many centuries of musical excellence are also young, relatively unheard of, and willing to push the envelope of the tradition they hold in trust for those who follow. Furthermore we make a conscious effort to present artists from the North Indian tradition on the same stage as artists from the Carnatic tradition, an innovation that is rare even in India. And outside the auditorium, marketing, the world wide web, new media, partnerships with more established institutions, like BBC Radio 3 and Sky, are key to reaching new audiences.

Darbar represents a recognition on the part of our team that we have a responsibility to take part in civil society, a realisation that there is more to being a good citizen than obeying the law of the land and paying taxes. We live in one community and as immigrant communities that resulted from Imperial expansion in times past we can make our ancestors' misfortune our bounty. We are as comfortable

listening to Mahler or Iggy Pop as we are listening to dhrupad; Shakespeare is as much our inheritance as Kalidasa and Bulleshah. We are incredibly fortunate not to have imbibed any of these cultures in a second-hand manner as scholars are often forced to do but were born into both the culture of the East and that of the West simultaneously. It is our responsibility to show the world through our good fortune that such divides are artificial and that this is an inheritance for all humanity to rejoice in.

So in the final assessment Darbar is important because it represents what our world can become: a multi-ethnic, multi-religious audience, many of whom are émigrés twice over, listening to music performed in praise of Hindu gods, Muslim saints or verses from the Sikh's Guru Granth Sahib, or nature and the beauty of life itself. The audience's diversity and range of musical tastes serves to remind us that ultimately, however we seek to define ourselves, our core identity, when everything that is of little importance is stripped away remains the same; a member of the human race.

Dr Debipriya Das
Tanpura / 2008

Ghatam
Carnatic percussion instrument

Pandit Ajoy Chakrabarty [khayal vocalist]
Raag Charukesi / 5th March 2008

Mysore A. Chandan [carnatic flute]
Raag Mohana / 14 April 2007

Artists and promoters believed that British audiences did not have the background, training and the cultured appetite to appreciate and digest classical music at its most refined and raw. Instead, performances were generally full of musical gymnastics, pyrotechnics and technical proficiency. **Sandeep Singh Virdee**

Pandit Rakesh Chaurasia
Backstage / 4th April 2008

Pandit Rakesh Chaurasia [bansuri]
Raag Prabatewashari / 4th April 2008

darbar
SOUTH ASIAN MUSIC FESTIVAL

ARTS COUNCIL
ENGLAND

Heritage
Lottery Fund

Phoenix Theatre
Leicester / April 2007

02
Darbar
South Asian
Music Festival

Author Jameela Siddiqi

"There was this wonderful, carefree feeling of being on a musical 'campus', a delicious feeling of being blissfully cocooned-off from the world, far away from trouble and strife and wars, a cushioned space where one lived, breathed and ate Indian classical music all day and night and while renewing friendships with fellow music lovers over and over again. **Jameela Siddiqi**

Jameela Siddiqi
Author

Inaugurated in 2006, the first Darbar Festival of South Asian music was a tribute to inspirational teacher and musician, Bhai Gurmit Singh Virdee – a highly respected and long-established resident of Leicester. The annual festival has, however, already started to feel like a long-established event with a select, devoted following of its own. No doubt, the Darbar team has worked, quite literally, day and night, to preserve the connotations of the word, 'Darbar', while at the same time transporting it into a thoroughly modern setting. It seems to me that they've managed to get this balance just right and the Darbar Festival may well become the prime event of Indian classical music outside of India.

Historically, 'Darbar' is associated with Indian royalty and its glittering assemblies of nobility and aristocracy-turned-statesmen. Business aside, one of the functions of the Darbar was that it served as the prime setting, and one to which every artiste aspired, for all that was the best of its kind in literature, (especially poetry), dance and music. In so doing, the Darbar itself became one of the chief arbiters of good taste in music, overseeing its development and evolution while at the same time providing a rigorous form of quality control through direct patronage of performing musicians. Although many of the rulers had not had any formal training in music, they had an extremely discerning ear and it wasn't at all unusual for some musician to be hauled up and given a dressing-down in the morning for having messed up on a raag the night before. The Royal sanction, serving as a badge of approval, was an essential prerequisite for a musician hoping to get anywhere in his field. Not surprisingly, particular styles of music known as 'gharanas' (literally, extended family) coincided with towns and cities which were centres of these semi-autonomous kingdoms and principalities.

Since the Darbar Festival concerns itself, mainly, with the classical music of India, (a music that was chiefly elitist), the event organisers seem particularly alert to preserving that exclusive classicism with one major difference: accessibility for all. For something to truly qualify as 'classical' it has to embody that timeless quality of the moment in which it was born with all the magic and mystique of ages past, yet it must also have a relevance in the present moment.

As a fully paid-up member of a twice-displaced Indian diaspora, (of Indian parentage, a mixture of north and south India, yet East African by birth and upbringing and now a Londoner for nearly 35 years), I've never felt closer to my Indian ancestry and heritage than when listening to dhrupad or khayal. Not surprisingly, for me, the Darbar Festival is by far one of the most satisfying musical events of its kind, a festival in the real sense, making it stand out from many others in which a series of disjointed concerts being held at different venues attempt, in vain, to pass off as a 'festival'. At Darbar 2007, held in its home city of Leicester, there was this wonderful, carefree feeling of being on a musical 'campus', a delicious feeling of being blissfully cocooned-off from the world, far away from trouble and strife and wars, a cushioned space where one lived, breathed and ate Indian classical music all day and night and while renewing friendships with fellow music lovers over and over again. And that's not just the festival audience. Every single sound engineer, photographer, camera-person as well as stage-hands and ushers, conveys an air of total belonging in a very special musical family.

There was also the added bonus of having easier access to the performers, well, easier than it would be at other events when maestros are more likely to remain concealed in their dressing-rooms. But, at Darbar, it was a common sight to see major, world-famous musicians mingling with listeners and

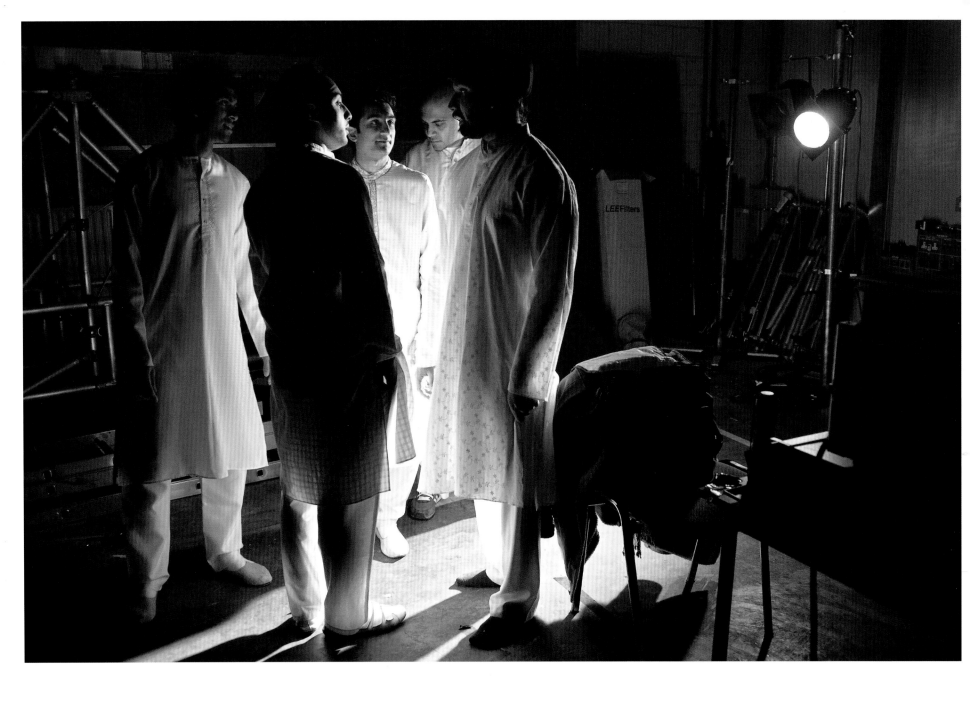

Backstage at the Peepul Centre
Darbar Festival / 2006

fans in the foyer or over a meal or cup of tea. More important, all the maestros were present at one another's performances, adding a whole new dimension to proceedings so that audiences didn't just get to see top-class performances, but also got to see, at first-hand, the reactions of all the maestros to one another's expertise. And neither was it just about maestros back-slapping praise on one another. They were all very much at hand to encourage and inspire lesser known, up-coming talents from home and abroad.

One of the most memorable moments from Darbar 2007 was the performance of tabla whizz kid Rimpa Shiv, a young woman trespassing on what is traditionally male territory, watched from the front row by every single big musician present for that year's Darbar, and the unanimity with which they shot up from their seats and the genuine affection which accompanied their standing ovation. Undoubtedly, a proud moment for Rimpa and her family. There can't be too many young Indian musicians, and female tabla players at that, who are given such a golden opportunity to perform before a front row of such big-name-and-fame vocalists and instrumentalists.

Most unusually, the maestros at Darbar had been contracted not only to perform at the festival but also to stay for its entirety and be part of all the other performances. Many musicians commented on the rarity of this arrangement and the fact that it was a relaxed change from their usual schedules, especially in India where, more often than not, it's a case of doing one quick show after which there's barely time to change before catching a flight to another city, another event. The sheer luxury of remaining at a festival for three full days meant a great deal of quality leisure time in which to catch up with one another. The maestros were all housed in the same hotel and, according to one of them, there were some terrific late-night gatherings, leading to intense inspiration and then some hard practising sessions aimed at impressing one another at the following day's recitals.

In keeping with the Indian classical tradition, however accomplished or distinguished a musician, long and hard practice sessions known as 'riyaaz' are the norm. Walking through the hallways of that hotel where the musicians were

(L-R)
Bhinderjeet Neer
Dharmesh Parmar
Gurprit Matharu
Harmeet Virdee
Amrit Rasiya
Rohit Mistry
Dharm Varia

staying was an almost surreal, and truly wonderful, experience, as different musical sounds emerged from behind each closed door: the distant beat of a tabla, the echoes of slide guitar, sitar, vocals – all merging into one exquisite stream, akin to the flow of liquid gold. To be in the midst of all this, as a listener and lover of classical music, there's an unmistakable feeling of belonging to something larger, and older (at least three thousand years, if not older) than the sum total of all those sounds and the exciting realisation that one is part of a living tradition and a rich heritage that is, even at this moment, in the process of evolution and that this is not happening at one of those old royal courts or in the private chambers of a nawab or maharajah but, right here, in 21st century Britain.

One of the best things about Darbar is that it features all Indian classical music. There is, really, only one Indian classical music, albeit of two different traditions. So far, at least in Britain, organisers have tended to mainly focus on North Indian classical music whereas Darbar has been vigilant in giving equal exposure to Carnatic (South Indian) music and its many exponents who are, as yet, not as well-known as their northern counterparts.

The two traditions, North and South, have come down to us through the same roots although their subsequent development and evolution have followed entirely different paths. Carnatic music, on the whole, has remained purer and true to its original form whereas Hindustani (or North Indian) music has absorbed many foreign elements, notably those of its Muslim (Turko-Persian-Moghul) rulers who held sway in northern India for something like 700 years.

Pandit Tejendra Majumdar
Sarod maestro

Bickram Ghosh and Pete Lockett
Backstage at Phoenix / 5th April 2008

Indians believe that music is of Divine origin so it's not really surprising that Indian classical music has its roots in devotional ritual, gradually emerging from the temples, via the royal courts and then, with the ending of royal patronage and the disbanding of kingdoms, onto the concert arena in India as well as abroad. But, even when it's being performed in a purely secular context, India's classical music has always retained its essentially devotional form so that even lighter classical vocal forms (like thumri or ghazal), often with ribald, flirtatious lyrics, still manage to convey to the listener, the feeling of a worship ritual.

All through Darbar, I found myself wondering whatever became of all those doom and gloom merchants of the early 20th century who had (quite wrongly) predicted that classical music was breathing its last, now that the kingdoms had disappeared and the talkies had arrived and, coupled with other western influences, film music had taken such a stranglehold over popular tastes. But, that's the beauty of India – the ability to absorb anything and everything and to let it be, side by side: bicycles and Cadillacs, breathtaking palaces-turned hotels and pavement dwellers right outside them, sophisticated technology and ancient labour-intensive occupations, Pandit Birju Mahraj and Helen, Pandit Bhimsen Joshi and Mohammed Rafi, Begum Parveen Sultana and Asha Bhosle (both of whom can, and do, often have the same fan base). Moreover, those who had predicted the decline of Indian classical music could not have foreseen the formation of sizeable (and largely prosperous) Indian communities settling in the West and yearning for their cultural roots. In post-independent India, the end of feudalism and the disbanding of kingdoms resulted in the decline of royal patronage which was gradually replaced by state/government and public patronage while Indian communities, whose numbers were swelling in Britain, Canada and the USA had come through their early struggles of immigration and established themselves well enough to turn their minds to art and culture. Both these processes played a vital part in propagating and ensuring the continuity of India's classical tradition.

Future historians of Indian music will cite the turn of the last century as the one in which classical Indian music gathered a large following outside of India. Perhaps they will also cite this as the time when both North and South Indian musicians began, in earnest, to listen to one another and to seek an interface. Alas, the 20th century will also be remembered for the partition of the Indian sub-continent with geo-political boundaries drawn up by British civil servants who, nevertheless, failed to partition Indian music. Even so, the 'wound' of partition certainly made itself felt in that it became increasingly difficult to make an impartial theoretical study of the history of Indian music as musicologists, both sides of the border, began to have many axes to grind. But, Indian music being the one area where knowing and feeling are entirely different concepts, those of us who loved this music were able to bypass the heavy-duty textbooks and just let the music wash over us.

To conclude on a personal note, I have reasons of my own for celebrating the birth of Darbar in Leicester – of all places. More than any other British city, Leicester has loomed large in my psyche for a very specific reason: just days after Uganda's then military dictator, Idi Amin, announced the expulsion of Asians (Indians) in August 1972, the leading national daily, Uganda Argus, carried a full page advert from Leicester City Council (or some such body) urging Ugandan Asians to choose a destination other than Leicester, if they were headed for Britain. I don't recall a reason being given but the implication was that Leicester was, already, too full up with Indians and that if any more were headed for Britian it would be better if they went to some other town or city.

It had really hurt to see this, so blatantly, in black and white – not that I was planning to go to Leicester, but many

Pandit Ramesh Mishra
Sarangi / 4th March 2006

Smt Kaushiki Chakraborty, Ranjana Ghatak & Dr Debipriya Das
A lighter moment / 5th April 2008

thousands of Ugandan Asians had assumed they would be joining relatives in Leicester. So, with 30 days to get out of the country and with a cash sum of only £50, and in some cases not even that, and every stick of your belongings left behind, imagine seeing an ad that basically amounted to being told that you were not welcome, at least in this one British city. Indians (and Pakistanis, for that matter) are extremely family oriented and in the trauma of losing everything and being kicked out of one's birthplace against a backdrop of terror and violence, the comfort of being able to join, at least to start off with, relatives already settled abroad, cannot be overemphasised. But Leicester was not exactly waiting with open arms.

Imagine my feelings, some 35 years on, when I stepped into Leicester for the very first time to attend what is set to become probably the biggest and best festival of Indian classical music outside of India. And to realise that the architects of this momentous event are none other than Ugandan, or at any rate, East African Asians, Asians twice removed from their heritage yet at the very forefront of its preservation and continuation.

Smt Kaushiki Chakraborty [khayal vocalist]
Raag Abhogi / 5th April 2008

Pandit Ravi Shankar Upadhay & Ustad Bahauddin Dagar
Morning chaa before the performance / 4th March 2006

Debojoyti Bose [sarod]
Raag Maduvanti / 5th April 2008

"Walking through the hallways of that hotel where the musicians were staying was an almost surreal, and truly wonderful, experience, as different musical sounds emerged from behind each closed door: the distant beat of a tabla, the echoes of slide guitar, sitar, vocals — all merging into one exquisite stream, akin to the low of liquid gold. Jameela Siddiqi

Neyveli Venkatesh
Mridangam / 4th April 2008

Pandit Nayan Ghosh and Ustad Irshad Khan
Backstage / 6th April 2008

Pandit Ramesh Mishra with Pandit Ronu Majumdar
Backstage / 5th March 2006

Pandit Uday Bhawalkar with Pandit Rakesh Chaurasia
Backstage / 4th April 2008

Bhai Baldeep Singh with Ustad Bahauddin Dagar
At the Peepul Centre / 4th March 2004

Pandit Subhankar Bannerjee with Pandit Tejendra Majumdar
Breakfast / 5th March 2006

Pandit Subhankar Bannerjee with Pandit Ronu Majumdar
Raag Bhoop / 5th March 2006

03
Shivir — Developing Artists

Author John Ball

"There is certainly no shortage of UK-based musicians with a passion for Indian music, many of whom have had to struggle through a self-financed education in vocal music, tabla and other Indian instruments. As far as I am aware, all of the UK-based South Asian musicians have had to develop themselves without the support systems that are commonplace for musicians in western classical music. John Ball"

John Ball
Author

Building on the success of their first South Asian Music Festival in 2006, the Darbar team took a leap of faith by incorporating an ambitious educational initiative into their 2007 festival, organising the UK's first 'Shivir' for sitar and tabla in Leicester.

The Tabla Shivir gave some of the UK's hottest tabla talents the opportunity to experience a week of intensive training under the watchful eye of Yogesh Samsi, one of India's most established tabla trainers. Alongside was the Sitar Shivir, led by Ustad Shahid Parvez, an internationally acclaimed sitar maestro from India. Stretching over five days, the retreat launched the second Darbar Festival, leading into a weekend of Indian music concerts featuring some of the finest exponents of Indian music from the UK and abroad.

Shivir, as a concept, has increased in popularity in India over the last few years. Most commonly associated with the practice of yoga and meditation, it is a practice-based intensive retreat focusing on the training and development of advanced students. In many ways, Shivir is a kind of modern-day adaptation of the traditional gurukul system where the aspiring music student traditionally spent a period of prolonged study, sometimes several years, under the same roof as their Guru. Modern-day work and study schedules are obviously not flexible enough to accommodate that kind of tradition, but the Shivir has the potential to provide students with regular high quality training which can act as a stimulus to their on-going learning.

Like many other tabla enthusiasts, most of my tabla education over the last fifteen years had come from infrequent often self-funded trips to India and sporadic lessons and workshops from visiting maestros on tour from India. I was looking forward to spending some quality time with a tabla maestro in a concentrated environment with no outside distractions. I also hoped to gain a qualified assessment and a clearer insight into my own progress to date.

Tabla player Yogesh Samsi first voiced the idea of the Shivir, based on several previous visits to the UK. Over that period, he has built a dedicated following of aspiring tabla students who admire and respect his thorough and systematic approach to learning. Yogesh himself spent twenty-three years training with Ustad Alla Rakha Khan, one of the most innovative and skilled tabla players of the twentieth century. Yogesh has been organising regular Shivir retreats in Pune and Mumbai for several years with his most devoted students. He had witnessed the great benefits and transformation achieved by the students there through this practice.

There is certainly no shortage of UK-based musicians with a passion for Indian music, many of whom have had to struggle through a self-financed education in vocal music, tabla and other Indian instruments. As far as I am aware, all of the UK-based South Asian musicians have had to develop themselves without the support systems that are commonplace for musicians in western classical music where schools, universities and conservatoires provide a well established infrastructure for music students. After reaching performing standard through all of their hard work and endeavours, they often face the prospect of being overlooked by promoters in favour of international artists who seem to carry more kudos.

Always looking for innovative and effective ways to take South Asian music forward in the UK, the Darbar Festival team took up the idea and integrated the Shivir into their 2007 Festival to build upon the legacy left by the late Bhai Gurmit Singh Virdee, who passed away in 2005. He laid the foundation for serious teaching in the field of tabla in the UK, contributing twenty-two years' service of teaching at the Leicestershire School of Music. Over that period, he had developed a unique methodology of teaching from beginners to advanced students, and put together his own material in books for his students.

The Shivir was open only to students with a track record of demonstrating an on-going commitment to the promotion of Indian music through performing and teaching, or students who have shown potential for success in this field through their musical endeavours to date. In all, seventeen students were accepted onto the Shivir covering an age range from fourteen to fifty. For the students, there was as much a sense of nervous anticipation as excitement on the first morning.

The aim of the Shivir was to build up mental and physical stamina through extended sessions of sustained practice in the presence of the teacher who carefully monitored all aspects of the pupil's playing. It included almost eight hours of hands-on 'Riyaz' or practice. Yogesh has composed sequences on the tabla based on syllables and phrases that make up the essential building blocks in the player's tabla vocabulary, specifically designed for students to incorporate into their daily practice routine. A typical day began with the group practising one of these sequences for two hours without any break, with the pace carefully monitored, an exercise in both mental and physical stamina as much as anything else. From my experience, it is a myth that you can go into a kind of 'meditational auto-pilot' while practising repetitive sequences. Riyaz requires a high level of concentration with sustained focus on sound production, dynamics and tempo control. It was a rigorous programme designed to test the courage of the most devoted of tabla enthusiasts.

Other sessions also included the teaching of traditional compositions from Yogesh's vast knowledge base giving the students an insight into the sheer depth of the

tabla repertoire built up over centuries through the guru-shishya (teacher-disciple) tradition. Central to the concept of Shivir training are some challenges associated with the most traditional aspects of tabla training. For example, students were not allowed to write down notes in the sessions or notate new taught material. All new material had to be memorised and was taught through the traditional practice of Parhant. This practice involves the vocalising of tabla syllables. Parhant develops the student's ability to internalise new material, thus sharpening the mental faculty. Through this practice, the student should be able to articulate the nuances of the taught composition, understanding its dynamics before playing on the instrument. The system of Parhant is critical in tabla learning, but in my experience is often neglected in teaching.

Also incorporated into the Shivir was an evening concert where the students had the opportunity to listen to Yogesh perform as an accompanist to sarod player, Ken Zukerman. Though there is a strong tradition of solo playing, the primary role of professional tabla players is to perform as an accompanist to instrumentalists or vocalists, so it is essential for students to develop a clear understanding of its role and its aesthetics, another area of study covered in the Shivir with several invaluable tips. The Shivir certainly reminds teachers that their own learning is an essential part of sustainability and growth in the UK tabla scene. Whilst the immediate benefit is for the participating artists, the long-term benefit lies with the students of the Shivir participants as this newly acquired knowledge is passed on. For some of the more mature students the Shivir had clearly awoken an appetite for a depth in their learning that had not been alive for some time.

As well as fulfilling the function of strengthening the bond between teacher and student, one could also feel the power of the shared experience amongst the participants. I know that many of the students, myself included, felt that they had been able to keep going for five days through the dynamic energy levels created by the group and the support that the more senior tabla players gave to those that had less experience. There is a vibrant tabla community in the UK covering the length and breadth of the country, which has been steadily gaining in strength over the last twenty years.

Nina Virdee [khayal vocalist]
Raag Ahir Bharav / 5th March 2006

Pandit Subhankar Bannerjee
adjusting his tabla

Pandit Nayan Ghosh with Pandit Purbayan Chatterjee
Shahbaz Hussain, Sukhwinder Singh and Sanju Sahai

However, it is rare to see seventeen of the UK's most dedicated and able tabla players spending five days under the same roof, engaged in shared learning experiences and having the time to discuss issues relating to their own development in detail. The strength in the bonds created was evident in the days following the Shivir at the festival, where all the participants sat down together to enjoy twenty-five hours of music performed by thirty artists over three days. In the breaks, you would see tabla players involved in animated discussions about the performances that they had witnessed and reflecting on the last five days of their training as the impact of the experience started to sink in.

It was evident that the students came away with a deeper understanding of their own musical path, a clearer picture of the challenges that lie ahead, and a stronger sense of the importance of quality learning built on systematic and well-conceptualised practice.

All the participants left the festival exhausted but at the same time exhilarated, and excited by the prospect that this could be the first of a sequence of Shivir retreats that would have a transformational effect on themselves and their music, at the same time bringing about a sea change in Indian music education in this country.

Pandit Yogesh Samsi [tabla]
Accompaniment / 15th April 2008

"I know that many of the students, myself included, felt that they had been able to keep going for five days through the dynamic energy levels created by the group and the support that the more senior tabla players gave to those that had less experience. John Ball"

Ustad Shahid Parvez Pandit Yogesh Samsi & Dr Debipriya Das
Raag Mian Ki Todi

Pandit Sanju Sahai & Pandit Ravi Shankar Upadhyay
Tabla & Pakhawaj Duet / 15th April 2007

Bhai Harjinderpal Singh [santoor]
Raag Bhopal Todi / 15th April 2007

04
A Passage
to Perform

Author Gurdain Singh Rayatt

" I remember the sweat 'raining' like a monsoon down Surojato's face, Kaushik's fingers punching a hole in his baya or bass drum and the black portion of my baya turning to liquid from the sweat on my arm.
Gurdain Singh Rayatt

Gurdain Singh Rayatt
Author

The art of tabla-playing is not a common thing in this world. Many people sit in wonder at how complicated the art actually is, yet others are blissfully unaware of its intricacies and liken it to the 'bongo'. In actual fact, the drum has evolved into the most versatile finger drum available on this planet. With the exploration of such an instrument, it is tradition and ground rules which provide the foundation for learning its complexities. As a tabla student practises, an intimate relationship grows between the student and the tabla, as he or she is held in a trance by the sounds resonating from the drum. But why is there this meditative discipline?

The mastering of the ground rules and tradition is always determined by the Guru (teacher) from whom you are learning. In a situation with multiple teachers, the developing style of the student's tabla-playing can easily be disturbed. In this case, one of the teacher's styles is adopted as a dominant style, in order to maintain a discipline in learning. As an audience member, the tabla student gets a glimpse of the wonderment of the instrument by senior maestros. In turn, the opinions of senior musicians add to the student's desire to practise and improve.

So it seems a tabla student practises for personal fulfilment and for the audience to which he or she may play. As more and more opportunities arise to perform, there are more people open to criticise or praise the student's abilities. The reputation of certain venues can sometimes instantly provide the student with a higher acclaim than previously. I would like to share my experience of performing at the Saptak Festival in Ahmedabad, a city in the Indian state of Gujarat, in January 2006. For me, it was a significant step in my development as a tabla performer and a chance to show that an art so deeply rooted in India, is still being maintained outside India.

Looking back to 2005, I had decided to take a year out in India to improve my tabla, before starting my degree at King's College London. I felt an urge to immerse myself into tabla and learn further from one of the most highly acclaimed tabla gurus around, Pandit Shankar Ghosh. India was a new experience. It was exciting and, at times, daunting, but with the music and tabla, I gradually became more comfortable in unfamiliar surroundings. The universal quality of the language of music, whichever genre, was something that I could express freely between my fellow guru-bhais ('brothers' learning from the same guru) and guru-behens ('sisters' learning from the same guru). I benefitted from living with a guru-bhai for the entire year. Surojato Roy was 16 and had been learning for almost 9 years. Kaushik Konwar, 23 and learning for the past 11 years, was also in the same house. Through group practice, we began to understand how tabla players communicate musically. It laid the foundation to becoming good friends.

Coming from England, we naturally compared our different learning experiences. Other students had been learning from Guruji (Pandit Shankar Ghosh) for a long time in their home country. I learnt from my father, Harkirat Singh and my grandfather, Bhai Gurmit Singh Virdee. From a young age, I would sit next to our hi-fi system for hours listening to Indian classical music, excluding myself from anything else around me. My grandfather learnt the Punjab style of playing the tabla from Ustad Bahadur Singh and later became a disciple of the great Pandit Samta Prasad where he continued his training under the Benares style of tabla. During my father's training, audio recordings were more widely available and in this way, he developed other styles of tabla-playing, with compositions from Lucknow and Farukhabad. By listening to many of my tabla idols from previous generations, I too had grasped a fair amount of compositions from each style on top of what my father and grandfather had taught me. This became very beneficial in Kolkata. Another benefit was learning from both Guruji and his son, Bikram Ghosh, during our summer schools and workshops in England. I had already become accustomed to the new notation and spelling systems that they both used to teach their students.

Guruji would teach his beginners with a great deal of focus on rhythmic discipline through Paranth (speaking of tabla phrases) and clapping to keep a sense of time. In practical training, he would concentrate on volume of the strokes before clarifying the correct hand movements. My father, however, would assert the correct hand position from day one, regardless of volume, which would come naturally through practice. I also realised that my father's students progressed more quickly with their ability to actually play the drum but all developed at a slower rate when rhythms became more difficult. In comparison, Guruji's students were able to deal with rhythmic variations much more easily because of their initial training but progressed more slowly with their physical abilities.

Guruji had a vision to create a tabla trio composition that would be unlike any other tabla performance around. Allowing the traditional elements to co-exist alongside experimental rhythm and tuneful melody, Guruji would create a piece that would be difficult to fault, appealing to all members of the audience, be it senior tabla enthusiasts, knowledgeable about tabla-playing, or the average music lover. As Guruji's vision came to fruition through his teachings, I was faced with the most intense and gruelling practice sessions of my entire life. Now and then, Guruji would make us sit and play his composition to monitor its effect and make improvements. However, we would all have to play in the scorching heat with all of the fans turned off. With all eyes on Guruji for approval, we would only notice a gentle pat of the right hand on his thigh to indicate that we must speed up! The suspense, the worry and the enjoyment were all acceleration factors in our struggle to coax a smile from our Guruji, an indication that we doing well.

At home we would practise from 10pm to 3am every day. Coordination, speed control and aesthetics of playing alongside stage presence were the most important things to consider for the composition because there were three of us. Naturally, we had to all keep up with the pace but the physi

cal exertions would leave us completely out of energy. One evening during a practice in front of Guruji, I remember the sweat 'raining' like a monsoon down Surojato's face, Kaushik's fingers punching a hole in his baya (bass drum) and the black portion of my baya turning to liquid from the sweat on my arm. After three or four small performances in and around Kolkata, Guruji's composition became longer and more difficult. The pressures and the on-going challenges Guruji imposed on our playing were being doubled every day as he would phone with a few words to enhance the piece.

As for Saptak, such a high class and prestigious opportunity would only be worth it, if our performance did the venue justice. Saptak did not begin as a festival but as the Saptak School of Music, inaugurated by the great Pandit Ravi Shankar in 1980. Following the same Guru Shishya Parampara (one-to-one relationship between student and teacher) style of teaching that I was experiencing with Guruji, the school still teaches sitar, sarangi, flute, violin as well as tabla and pakhawaj. The expansion into performing can be seen as a worthwhile bridge for students to learn about aesthetics and presentation, watch great artists perform and provide opportunities for students to perform.

As it turned out, back in January 2005, my grandfather, Bhai Gurmit Singh Virdee had decided to organise a family outing to the Saptak Festival with my parents, my uncles and my aunts. It had always been a dream for him to go and see an Indian classical festival in India and revel in the music playing all day long. Unfortunately, he passed away two months later without having made the trip. While in Kolkata, my uncle Sandeep was planning the first Darbar Festival for

Gurdain in the fast lane
Ahmedabad, Gujurat, India

In conversation with Bhai Baldeep Singh
Jori – Heritage of Punjab percussion / 4th March 2008

2006 as a tribute to Gurmit Ji and queried whether I could play at the Saptak Festival 2006 through the Darbar Artist Exchange Programme.

Not only was the performance an appreciation of Guruji's versatile creativity and a celebration of his teaching but it became a personal tribute to my grandfather to not only fulfil his dream of attending the festival but also to be able to perform on the famous Saptak stage in his memory. The Darbar Exchange Programme continues to open up opportunities for UK artists. Dharambir Singh performed the sitar at the 2007 Saptak Festival and Nina Virdee performed in 2008.

Once the opportunity to perform at Saptak came our way, we could not believe that we would be able to sit on the same stage as countless other top-class maestros. Looking at the programme, the pleasure of seeing our names alongside greats such as Ustad Zakir Hussain, Pandit Hariprasad Chaurasia, Pandit Ajoy Chakraborty was amazing but also terrifying. After a hectic journey to Mumbai and then a delayed and stressful flight to Ahmedabad, with countless pieces of luggage and nine drums in hard cases, we settled in our hotel and relaxed for an hour or so. We made a quick trip to the Saptak venue and arrived exactly as Zakir Ji walked to sit on stage with Hariprasad Ji. Their performance was warm and intimate and a good taste of how the venue would feel as we sat on stage in a few days to come. Kaushik and Surojato were even more astounded, as this was their first opportunity to watch and meet Zakirji in person. After the concert, we informed him that we were performing a few days later and he bade us good luck before rushing away amongst a crowd of fans. We felt blessed further when he unexpectedly stopped his car on the way out of Saptak to shake our hands and wish us all the best for our performance.

During the next few days, the three of us were sat in concentrated practice in our hotel room, ordering food continuously to keep us energised. A few walks around Ahmedabad permitted some fresh air and a chance to explore but then a swift return to our practice ensued, with Guruji still phoning from Kolkata to alter the composition!

On the morning of the performance, all was quiet and calm as we proceeded to the festival. We had a practice room at the back of the venue to sit and tune our tablas before the concert,

but within minutes we had locked ourselves in. The lock was broken and we were in laughter at how quickly such a panicked situation had occurred. Fortunately, we were helped out from our temporary imprisonment in time to go onto the stage.

The performance progressed smoothly, with appreciative gestures from the audience. The experience was uplifting but also calming. We all realised that the extensive practice had earned us our determined stage appearance and our confidence. Starting with a shuruaat (slow development piece), we moved onto various compositions involving difficult phrases such as dheredhere (involving the swinging of the right palm). Each piece worked on a different number of microbeats, adding a complexity to the performance that tabla enthusiasts would appreciate. The addition of the third drum and the melodious tuning of the instruments resulted in an almost trance-like experience even for us on stage.

After the performance, to our amazement, people were asking for our autographs. One audience member was even touching Kaushik's feet as a sign of respect. Backstage, Yogesh Samsi, a disciple of late Ustad Alla Rakha smiled and shook his head in appreciation of the performance, which alone is a great response from a respected tabla player. After watching Ustad Rashid Khan perform with Yogeshji, we returned to our hotel, exhausted. The day after, we returned back to Kolkata and were invited to perform at the festival again next year. Unfortunately however, due to university education, there was no time for us to meet up to practise for the piece or perform the year after.

We were not finished nonetheless: a few weeks after our return, Guruji altered the composition once more for a mehfil (small home concert) during Saraswati Puja and again

for a final concert in Kalyani, outside Kolkata in February. Even today, the art of playing the tabla is always changing, the journey never-ending and the experience everlasting!

The experience of travelling to Ahmedabad and performing in the Saptak Festival is one I will not forget. I'm glad that through practice and advanced training, this beautiful art can be maintained in such a technologically-driven world as ours and that through further exposure, future generations can keep the heritage of this instrument alive. In this millennium we have already seen the tabla branch out into at least three distinct directions. The more mainstream western pop and hip-hop producers have sampled loops of the instrument to add an Indian flavour to their tracks. Famous tracks include Missy Elliot's hit 'Get Ur Freak On' and Britney Spears sampled a tabla cycle in her song 'My Prerogative'. Other tabla players have become the torch-bearers for the traditional and pure classical form of the tabla, the role models for the current generation to look up to - maestros such as Pandit Kumar Bose, Pandit Anindo Chatterjee, Pandit Swapan Chaudhuri and, of course, Ustad Zakir Hussain. Thirdly, there are those musical experiments that are conducted between these two branches, with the purpose of blending the traditional culture of Indian classical music alongside the influences of world and western music. Talvin Singh and Nitin Sawhney are prime examples of artists fusing South Asian cultural heritage and their British sensibilities. Let us all work together to keep this musical form alive.

Harkirat & Gurdain Singh Rayatt
Father and son

Tabla Trio: Gurdain, Kaushik & Surojato
Saptak Festival / January 2006

Each piece worked on a different number of microbeats, adding a complexity to the performance that tabla enthusiasts would appreciate. The addition of the third drum and the melodious tuning of the instruments resulted in an almost trance-like experience even for us on stage. **Gurdain Singh Rayatt**

Smt. Rimpa Shiv [tabla]
Solo in Teental / 13th April 2007

05
Heritage

Author Dr Ranjeev Singh Bhangoo

Dr Ranjeev Singh Bhangoo
Author

I was asked to write an article on heritage in Indian classical music and being neither a writer nor an expert on Indian classical music readily agreed. Sober reflection has led me to regret this decision and by way of apology I begin by offering an explanation of why in a fit of self delusion I accepted the offer.

I was about five, certainly no more, and the noise coming from the reel-to-reel via the speakers was not from the world as I knew it. Nothing I had heard so far in life made me stop and listen; I mean actually listen rather than just use the music as the soundtrack to a five-year-old's life. A series of low-pitched vocalisations that gradually sped up over a period of a few minutes and then acquired a rhythm and later a drum accompaniment and eventually became exceedingly fast before ending. From time to time I would ask my father to find the piece and put it on again for me. If I ever made the mistake of doing this in front of my cousins after a few minutes of bewilderment they would do an impression of the singers; this mostly involved constipation as the motivating factor behind the music. This was obviously a lone pursuit. And then one day the tape broke and that was that.

Two or three years later and I find a forgotten LP in my father's collection with a musician sitting cross-legged and holding a strange instrument, later discovered to be a sitar, on the cover. Putting it on and listening there were a series of strokes without rhythm gradually picking up pace and then a drum came in, eventually the playing became fast, faster even than Jimmy Page and then a crescendo and silence. It reminded me of the music I had listened to on the reel-to-reel a few years ago, sure he played a sitar and didn't sing but he was basically doing the same thing and the end result was the same; he made me stop and listen. I wanted more but where from? This was the only LP of the type we had and we didn't know anyone who knew a thing about Indian classical music.

You will excuse the fact that I didn't think of it as 'South Asian classical music'; a child's enthusiasms are seldom couched in politically correct terms.

Then an Indian record shop opened and I found a box set of four LPs labelled Indian Classical Music – Vocal. At home there was even more good news: the box contained a booklet with information on each artist, pictures and a glossary. I put on what I now knew to be Ustad Amir Khan singing a raga called Darbari Kanada in the khayal style; the piece originally composed for the Mughal Court and meant to convey feelings of majesty. The voice rose up from nowhere, sounding as though it had never belonged to an individual living in a given time period, so outside of such facile notions it stood. Each phrase fully formed and conveying the majesty, paranoia, loneliness and ultimate futility inherent in the wielding of power. John Donne was right when he said 'no man is an island' but then he hadn't heard the loneliness, the distance from common humanity conveyed in this piece. There was no singing in the normal sense of the word: it was as though the artist was talking but in perfect tune and with perfect timing; and the timing was the key thing, his silences were eloquent. At times he seemed almost apologetic to interrupt the majestic profound silences, he was an architect building an edifice with simple pure clean lines: the material he was working with was silence, the spaces of silence, enclosed by walls of sound. The meaning, the life of the house he built was contained within these rooms, in the silence. At the end of the LP I sat there for a few minutes as the needle continued to turn in the groove at the end.

Side two, a big, fat happy-looking chap with an impressive handlebar moustache, alias Ustad Bade Ghulam Ali Khan, singing Raga Malkauns. Totally different, the booklet told me this was a romantic raga and he didn't disappoint; one moment his voice and tempo communicated the absolute

"The voice rose up from nowhere, sounding as though it had never belonged to an individual living in a given time period, so outside of such facile notions it stood. Each phrase fully formed and conveying the majesty, paranoia, lonelines s and ultimate futility inherent in the wielding of power.
Dr Ranjeev Singh Bhangoo

Bhai Baldeep Singh
Vocal / 3rd March 2006

ecstasy of being in love and having it returned, bubbling over with an ebullience barely in control; the next the absolute depths of anguish at the death of love. No silences here the artist was full of life and he had to tell you about it in its entirety. All this with the tenderest voice you ever heard, skating on the knife edge between emotional depth and a sweet mawkish sentimentality but never making the fatal slip, never putting his ego between the listener and the music, never aiming to flatter with musical conceits. This from someone who looked like a contented, bourgeois patriarch as opposed to a jilted lover.

These two pieces remain my 'gold standard' for excellence; is a piece of music good or really good? Does its impact on me come close to that of those two pieces or not? A simple enough test, Interpol's 'Slow Hands' passes, 'Sam's Town' by The Killers doesn't; good but not nearly good enough.

The other legacy was the booklet, for the first time I had the beginnings of a context, fertiliser for my personal heritage. It was now that I learnt how this form of music, khayal, started in late 18th century North India and evolved from an earlier form of singing, dhrupad, a style that was now apparently extinct. Further back this music had its own aesthetic theories of how certain pieces suited certain times and produced specific emotional resonances in the listener (and not just love or wonder but lust, fear, rage etc; the full gamut of emotions available to humankind). Later a suggestion that in the area where history merges with myth this music ultimately had its roots in Vedic chanting where sound without formal nominative meaning was used to articulate the unutterable: humanity's relationship with creation. These themes still ran as strong undercurrents in the modern forms perhaps explaining why so many of the great artists in this tradition became self-destructive as in their minds their art fell so far short of what they wished to express, the undercurrent pulling them under the waves to their doom.

Trips to the record shop brought new purchases and new insights; I learnt khayal had several different gharanas, 'demographic schools or styles of music', that emphasised different aspects of the performance such as time-keeping, rhythm, voice quality or the poetry that was sung but all with

the same aim; to achieve that emotional resonance in the listener. This information and new music, new to me at least but usually by a long-dead artist was like looking through a small break in the corner of a blacked-out window into a large derelict building; I could see just enough to frustrate.

The ensuing years followed the same pattern, the sporadic discovery of a new piece and the painful, slow, haphazard accumulation of knowledge with an occasional flash of lightning illuminating a broad unexplored vista and always in the background the semi-mythical dhrupad; no music to listen to just the occasional name or story.

Two bolts of lightning: the 'Agra gharana' and a tabla solo, by Pandit Anindo Chatterjee, on a deliberate oversize set. The 'Agra gharana', singers who sang in deliberately gruff, nasal, masculine voices that were anything but sweet but who produced the most moving music. Singers who defied you to see past the sound to the feeling underneath; who by sticking to the virtues of immaculate time-keeping and use of rhythm, allegedly virtues of the long-dead dhrupad, made you realise that great art is not about being pretty or just catching the feeling of the moment but is something that dislocates you from time and place, asking far more questions than it answers. The tabla solo slow, deliberate, the noise from the oversize drums (b flat as opposed to c sharp) rising up to the ears as if from the bottom of a well, full of echo and slightly muffled, the deliberate opposite of the razor-sharp lightning-fast drumming so in vogue. The drumming doing something I did not think percussion could do; conveying emotions other than excitement, in this case feelings of timelessness, repose,

Nina Virdee & Pandit Ramesh Mishra
Backstage / 5th March 2006

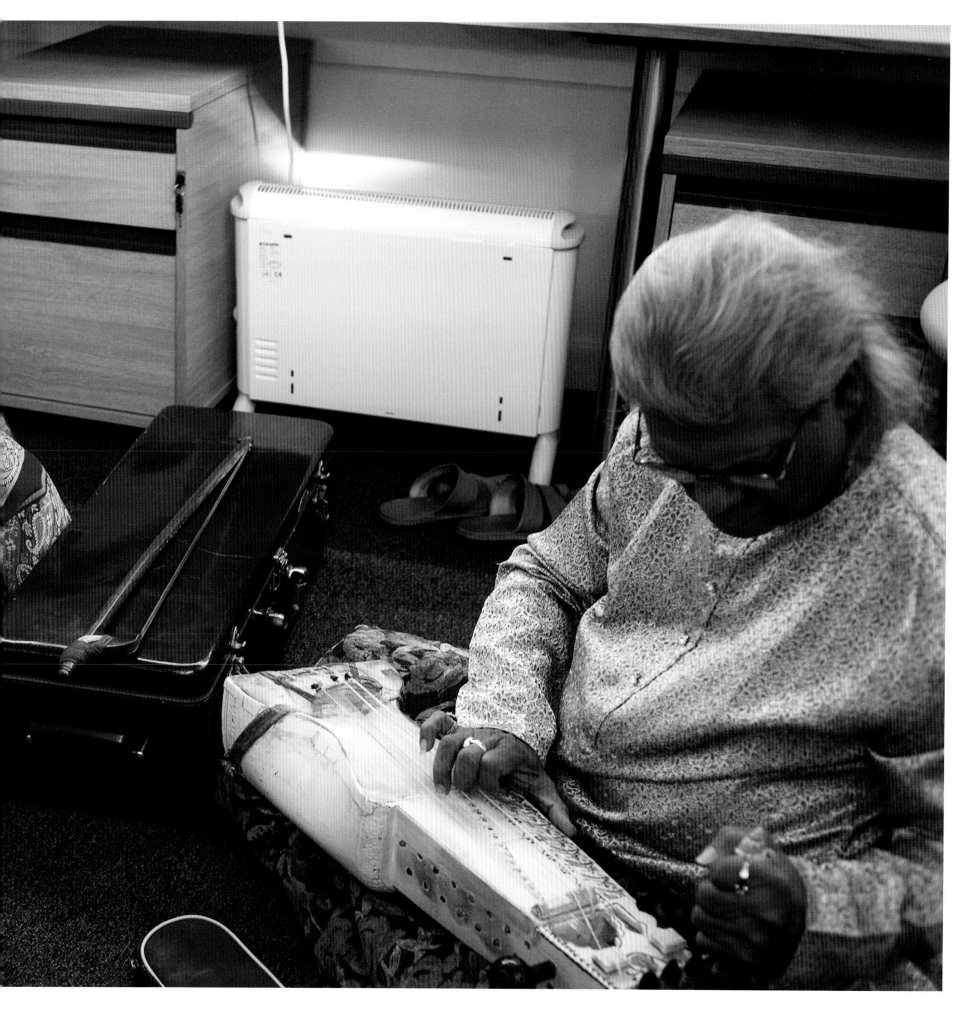

calm and introspection. Then the casual remark that this drumming was a deliberate attempt to emulate the subtle, almost unassuming sound of the double-ended pakhawaj used to accompany dhrupad added to a sense of frustration at an opportunity lost.

And then out of the blue Pandit Siya Ram Tiwari singing Raga Darbari Kanada in dhrupad. Putting on the LP all that I had read about dhrupad seemed to be inadequate. The richness of the timbre, the verve of the unaccompanied voice and then the low rolling accompaniment of the pakhawaj; singer and drummer in perfect unison, not missing a beat. The singer making no compromise to his art in an attempt to please the audience. This was art, not entertainment, no vocal theatrics, no sulphurous pyrotechnics with the percussion; austerity and discipline the touchstones of this music. The artist demanding of the listener that he or she make the effort to meet him on ground of his choosing, his art unsullied by fashion or the search for popularity. This was when I really first started to appreciate the importance of the 'bandish', the poetry that went with the music: the cadence, rhythm and subtle meaning of the words adding to the 'Rasa', the emotion of the piece. From that time on the discovery of new artists and styles such as the carnatic tradition of South India and the thumri have provided further delight.

So what is the heritage of Indian classical music as I see it; someone of Indian descent, born in England, currently living in Paris for a year trying to improve my feeble French; with a haphazard and irregular exposure to the music I have grown to love? Tolerance, plurality and integrity are the words that have always come to mind to describe this still living tradition.

Yes, this music had its origins in religion and continues to use hymns dedicated to gods and goddesses in its poetry, but ultimately the non-sectarian deity worshipped by all these artists is beauty; this is why it is so common to hear a Muslim singer singing a verse in worship of a Hindu deity, the poem often composed by the same artist. The same reason explains why the relationship between teacher and pupil, often closer than the relation between parents and their child, so key to the North Indian gharana system, sees teachers and pupils of different faiths come together. There is no Hindu tradition,

there is no Muslim tradition, there is just the tradition. As Bade Ghulam Ali Khan, a Muslim khayal singer who lived in India after partition, said "If every child in India had some knowledge of Indian classical music partition would never have occurred." Wishful thinking perhaps, but emphasising the unifying and plural heart of this tradition. Perhaps I can illustrate this point with what sounds as a contradiction in this context; the religious music of the Sikhs. This classical lineage traces its heritage back to Bhai Mardana, the constant companion of the first Sikh Guru, Guru Nanak Dev Ji. Bhai Mardana, a Muslim, is the acknowledged father of a tradition that sees the Sikh scriptures (writings composed by Sikh Gurus with some verses by Muslims Pirs and Hindu Sadhus) sung in a classical form. His followers, Rababis, occupying that beautiful space between religions, in this case Sikh and Muslim, continued to sing in Gurudwaras until 1947. This music refuses to succumb to arbitrary man-made divisions, rather as all great art it pulls people together.

Dhrupad, the keystone of the tradition, is a direct product of the impact of the Muslim Arabic and Central Asian traditions on the pre-existing Hindu traditions; the names Swami Haridas, Gopi Nayak and Mia Tansen (born Hindu but a convert to Islam) and its close relationship to the Mughal court tell you that this is a syncretic tradition. This interplay continued with the evolution of the sarod (a type of lute) from the central Asian rabaab, and the apocryphal role the great Indian Muslim renaissance man, Amir Khusrau, played in the evolution of the sitar from the original veena.

The music remains alive and continually evolving, each generation of artists inventing and reinterpreting the tradition for themselves, often visiting the still living wellspring of dhrupad for inspiration. These artists are not constantly looking over their shoulder burdened by a past that causes them to stumble and fall on the path they forge: rather this inheritance is like the clear, invigorating light of an early summer morning, a prism that literally casts old familiar objects into a new light. Some of the latest generation of dhrupad exponents have returned with vigour and passion to one of the very earliest interests of Indian musicians; the exploration of microtones, the smallest of intervals separating

Nina Virdee [khayal vocalist]
Raag Ahir Bharav / 5th March 2006

Anubrata Chatterjee
New Talent / 2nd March 2006

one note from another in an almost mystical pursuit of the smallest atoms of human emotion.

Today in search of this music I can turn to Google, YouTube or my iPod where on my commuting playlist a dhamar sitting next to Bruce Springsteen feels natural in the context of my life experience. This unparalleled access also extends to artists, accelerating the process of cross-fertilisation necessary for any tradition to remain vital and relevant. We have gone from the three-minute wax cylinder recordings of a Zora Bhai Agrawalli to a ten minute clip on YouTube. Yet the same rules apply: if the artist is good enough, time constraints do not serve as an impediment but rather a spur to his or her muse.

This remains a classical tradition however, and for it to achieve its aims and fulfil its potential it must retain a certain discipline and austerity if it is not to fall over into sentimentality. This does not mean rigidity, does not mean stupefaction, or a blind adherence to what went before, but a shunning of tricks and musical gymnastics; an acceptance that restraint often heightens, rather than lessens, a sentiment.

It must also remain an engaged art, as well as an art of abstraction, concerned with the ebb and flow of 'everyday' society, able to offer solace at times of distress and yet also capable of removing the blinkers of self-regard that can descend as the individual attempts to forge a career, find financial security and secure a future for their family. One aspect of this engagement with the audience that is perhaps unique is the interaction between audience and musician seen at live concerts, the audience expressing their appreciation of a particular musical phrase by spontaneous exclamations

during the recital, the artist often responding by repeating or elaborating the phrase. This perception of the audience as engaging in a dialogue with the music to produce a fully realised artistic experience, as opposed to being passive paying recipients of a hermetically sealed, hallowed artistic endeavour, which speaks only for the artist, is one of the enduring glories of this heritage.

But, ultimately to this listener, in the final reckoning, it remains an inheritance of generosity and humanity for all human-kind that because of its continued attempts to address the individual's relationship to the universe, remains capable of capturing the imagination of a five-year-old living in 1970s Britain and engendering a lifelong passion that has allowed him to appreciate Dylan, Robert Johnson and Monteverdi as well the glories of dhrupad and khayal.

Bhai Sukhwinder Singh
Tabla & Jori / 4th April 2008

Ustad Irshad Khan [surbahar]
Raag Darbari Kanara / 4th April 2008

Pandit Uday Bhawalkar [dhrupad vocalist]
Raag Gawoti / 6 April 2008

0:15:50:20
EC LOCK

Pandit Prem & Prashant Mallick [dharbanga dhrupad]
Raag Shudh Sarang & Bhimpalasi / 13th April 2007

"All that I had read about dhrupad seemed to be inadequate. The richness of the timbre, the verve of the unaccompanied voice and then the low rolling accompaniment of the pakhawaj; singer and drummer in perfect unison, not missing a beat. The singer making no compromise to his art in an attempt to please the audience. This was art, not entertainment, no vocal theatrics, no sulphurous pyrotechnics with the percussion; austerity and discipline the touchstones of this music. Dr Ranjeev Singh Bhangoo"

"There's nothing quite like the Darbar festival, not even in India... Darbar is unique in that it takes in all of Indian classical music. It's more usual to hear North Indian classical music in Britain but at Darbar the leading styles of Carnatic are also right at the heart of the festival. BBC Radio 3, World Roots"

Sanjay Subramanyan [carnatic vocal]
4th April 2008

Ustad Shahid Parvez [sitar]
Raag Rageshree / 15th April 2007

06

Indian Music, British Youth

Author Soumik Datta

'Sanskar' which is a complicated Hindi word that encapsulates a sense of culture, upbringing, decorum and aesthetics is what the older generation believe their successors have irreclaimably forfeited. **Soumik Datta**

Soumik Datta
Author

Centuries have passed since the heavily mythologised Tansen and the sumptuous opulence of the Moghul Empire. And decades after the era of patronage when live music resonated within the walls of decadent, candle-lit chambers, Indian classical music still stands today as the weather-beaten grandfather of musical genres. But in an age dominated by technology, pop culture, Americanisms and war, what place does this beautiful ancient art form hold? What relevance does it have to a generation obsessed by celebrities and iPods? And in particular what does Indian music have to do with the youth of Britain? Having studied Indian classical music whilst living in the UK, I found myself incorporated into a small fraternity here. This article is informed by my experiences within this community: their hopes, their concerns and their relentless passion for a heritage that is worth fighting for.

In the summer of 1996 I heard Dr William Radice speak at SOAS about a phrase that is perhaps most associated with appreciating Indian classical music. 'Kya Baat Hai' is a Hindi expression used by Indian audiences to convey their satisfaction for the music being performed. He explained that it was a standard utterance of appreciation that listeners called out mid-performance when moved by a particular nuance or musical phrase. A mature listener would recognise these spots in a concert and associate them with euphoric emotion or what he identified as the nine rasas.

As universal concepts, they have avatars in disparate traditions around the world. We find them in the Roman Catholic Church's division of the seven deadly sins and their corresponding seven holy virtues. Plato's Republic discusses the Four Cardinal Virtues. Dante's Divine Comedy bases itself around the nine Circles of Hell. Even the works of Chekhov and Stanislavski discuss particular emotional frames or rasas. However, Bharata Muni's Natyasastra argues that they are best represented when translated through an artistic Indian medium. Indeed, it is often concurred that every medium, be it classical architecture, sculpture, painting, literature, music or dance, shares the underlying beliefs of the nine rasas that inform the Indian religio-philosophical mind. I would argue that this aesthetic is at the very heart of appreciating Indian culture. And it is here that we must question how far my generation of Asian youths in Britain are from appreciating this aesthetic.

Swamped in a double-click, post-modern world, surrounded by a luminous army of media, pop music, technology and football, do they have any reason to feel part of a distant and spiritual world? Where first generation migrants lived their lives at crossroads between the economic boons of the developed world and nostalgic sentimentality for their motherland, second generation British Asians face different issues. For them, Britain is their birthplace. Their passports pronounce them as legal citizens of the United Kingdom. This is their motherland. Rather, India with its mumbo jumbo religio-philosophical aesthetics is foreign and one step removed from their everyday realities. It is the language of parents, dub-uncles and aunties who use it to explain superstitious concepts like fate, reincarnation and déjà vu and their connection with spirituality, peace and the artistic ethos. How much of this tradition has the next generation imbibed? Living amidst a population where larger numbers of people celebrate independence, celebrity, consumerism, amongst other excesses, it is vital to ask this: are British Asians more British or are they more Indian?

On asking the older Asian generation to comment on this, I was met with a unanimous voice that choroused 'more British'. Viewed from their perspectives, the new batch has lost its roots. They speak a different dialect pockmarked with colloquialisms and slang. Their accent is neither British nor Indian. They may never fear baring their bodies but nor do they promote the very colour of the skin they reveal. Indeed this colour that once stood blood-smeared as a force against white oppression now ironically disguises itself to appear more white. 'Sanskar' which is a complicated Hindi word that encapsulates a sense of culture, upbringing, decorum and aesthetics is what the older generation believe their successors have irreclaimably forfeited.

I consider this grossly untrue and misrepresentative of the British Asian populace. For if this was the case how could we

explain the rise of the Asian Underground movement in the mid-90s? If the British Asian mentality was incapable of capacitating the Indian aesthetic, what gave birth to the likes of Talvin Singh and Nitin Sawhney? Today, the UK and London in particular is responsible for generating and giving platforms to some of the world's biggest Indo-Fusion musical acts. Even against America's Karsh Kales and Anoushka Shankars, Britain has spawned an entire bloodline of Asian performers including M.I.A. Asian Dub Foundation, Sri, Rishi Rich Project, Raghav and others. The British Asian psyche never forfeited its 'Sanskar'. It merely developed newer ways of appreciating and adapting to it.

By the late 1980s, there was a silent but consented feeling amongst those who were interested in the development of music in Britain that the era of the World/New Age genre had outlived its time. A small collective of DJs, musicians and producers who were all ethnically from Asia (mainly Pakistan and India) but were making underground, DnB and dance music in the UK realised that by an intelligent synthesis of eastern and western rhythms surmounted by a solid, modal melody, they were able to create a new music with a distinctly ethnic feel. Asian Dub Foundation's 'Facts and Fictions' and Fun Da Mental's 'Seize the Time' were some of the oldest spearheads of this movement. By the time Talvin Singh produced 'Soundz of the Asian Underground', the definitive album that coined the genre in 1997, the eardrums of the British Asian youth were already resonating with a sound that immediately enhanced their subconscious understanding of the Indian aesthetic. Through the music, they began experiencing a psycho-sonic link with their homelands. The unique ensemble of rhythmic percussion and raag-based soundscapes created a space, midway between the music of Britain and India that celebrated their existence as a hybrid community.

The sonic language of these tracks was at once British, Asian, contemporary and its universal appeal meant that the youth of Britain listened with complete and unadulterated pride. Suddenly, the fashion community spoke of kitsch designs of Bollywood films on handbags and shoes. Indian pashminas became the defining characteristic of teenage haunts such King's Road and Sloane Square. That which had been labelled Asian and melodramatic turned into

Kamaljeet Ajimal
Santoor player

Bhinderjeet S Neer [tabla]
Tabla student / 3rd March 2006

the 'In' or the 'Retro'. Indeed, the escalation of the Indian hype encompassed a range of fields leading towards the birth of new age British-Indian cuisines, Brit-Indian cinema and a whole array of jobs, clothing, magazines and accessories to suit this new breed of people.

Running parallel to this movement was the Bhangra pop scene. Essentially the same principles applied. Bally Sagoo from Birmingham began remixing traditional Bhangra music with house, reggae and hip-hop. Armed with his spiky coiffure, he erupted a craze amongst Punjabis in the UK. His music continued its assault on mainstream culture until the bold strike of the Bhangra drum turned into a sonic icon that represented Punjab giving millions of NRI (Non-Resident-Indian) Punjabi youths in the UK a reason to celebrate their twofold identities.

Amidst the celebrations and all the escalating bravado in the UK, there was one community of Indian musicians who still had very little in common with the youth of Britain. And if this situation persevered, it would ultimately result in the demise of the art form within the country. Indian classical music was not music for the masses. Regarded as a discipline that necessitated time, years of effort and dedication, many were known to be exhausted by it, fear it or give up on it. In return, however, the music of the ancient ragas promised to far exceed the effects of contemporary music, mind-numbing dance beats or even the illegal psychedelics that often accompanied such environments. Indeed, it promised to make your soul dance.

Navras, the Asian Music Circuit and Milapfest can all lay claim to the golden years when large-scale Indian classical music concerts were held in this country. Today, the Darbar Festival hosts an incredible line up of maestros and younger artists. Where it is true that Hindustani classical music is best saved for small venues, baithaks or soirees, it is only through large-scale marketing and the organisation of festivals that the mainstream world can recognise that the classical genre exists and is still at large in the UK.

Moreover let us consider that it is inherently embedded in the spirit of the younger generations to be impressed by what they see and hear. But without a mainframe infrastructure that supports quality musicians and exposes them to the younger generations, the general population will remain oblivious to

this rich heritage. If we are to change with the times and play the games of the new generation, we must deploy newer toys. MySpace and iTunes along with the many labyrinths of the Internet must be utilised to their fullest extent. Animation films along the lines of Disney's 'Fantasia' should be made to dhrupad and khayal. Xbox and Playstation games should feature the classical music of India. What is needed is the stir or the hype that sends a powerful chain of waves rippling through the globe. Conversely, what we do not need is the air of elitism that surrounds classical music. Gone are the days of mehfils and guni-juns. Today, schools and universities must be targeted with a marketing strategy that accommodates the sex appeal of the new generation (without adulterating the purity of the music).

For those concerned about bringing an entirely seated, drone-based, deep and meaningful performance to a restless, beer-guzzling, British university community please revisit the BBC award-winning performances for World Music by Debashish Bhattacharya and Kaushiki Chakrabarty. There can be no debate that Indian classical music can be breathtaking to watch. The sheer age of the musical form that stretches centuries concedes to this. Those who disagree or remain indifferent are merely dim, vapid, woollen-headed zealots who have never witnessed the bejewelled, topaz-lit spectacles that are Ustad Zakir Hussain, Pandit Ajoy Chakrabarty and Ustad Ali Akbar Khan in performance.

Of course, the truth is that the prospects of popularising Indian classical music are few and far beyond. The process will be painfully slow. We can only pray that our children's children will listen with the same levels of sensitivity when they attend

all-night Indian classical concerts at the Proms or at Womad or on hot, summer Sundays in a jam-packed Hyde Park.

However, as we inch towards this day, I appeal to the British Asian youth to try to expose themselves to even small doses of pure classical music. Today, all Indo-Fusion music that keeps our youth happy in clubs and music festivals derived from the giant library of Indian classical repertoire that existed years before our time. Without it, the long catalogue of British Asian Music sub-genres would be obsolete. There is a long and meandering road ahead and there is space for many more to join our modest company.

In the spring of 2006, in a small basement studio outside Leeds, a group of five young friends confronted this truth. They decided that they too wanted to contribute to the cause. Being lovers and students of the classical form, they discovered that strong raga-based compositions could be aptly arranged in ways that replicated diverse World Music genres. And so they set about composing, arranging and recording an album where each track exposed Indian classical music through the filter of samba, reggae, jazz, hip-hop, blues, folk and flamenco. A goody bag of sorts, there was something for everyone. And even those who could not appreciate the intricacies marvelled at the range of colours. They hit the road, touring for some time winning every audience they played to. Not only were the tracks noticeably reggae or samba, but they came with an added flavour: a sweeping undercurrent of Indian classical melody, subconsciously banging on the psyches of a larger, more diverse audience. I am proud to be part of this band. It is a joy to work with what I consider the cream of the British Asian music world. It is an even greater joy to see the faces of the British diaspora animated by the exultant force of an essentially acoustic sound.

As we venture into an age that continues to classify music practising what Nitin Sawhney disdainfully dubs 'record shop apartheid', it is the duty of our band, Samay, and many other Samays that follow in time to ensure that the future of the Indian classical genre does not stagnate under the meaningless bracket of World Music. It deserves a shelf of its own and it is in the capable hands of the new generations of Indians living abroad to achieve this.

Kiranpal Singh [santoor]
Raag Bilaskhani Todi / 5th March 2006

Kaviraj Singh
Tanpura / April 2008

Today, all Indo-Fusion music that keeps our youth happy in clubs and music festivals is derived from the giant library of Indian classical repertoire that existed years before our time. Without it, the long catalogue of British Asian Music sub-genres would be obsolete. **Soumik Datta**

Pandit Bickram Ghosh and SUNEV musicians

Surdarshan S Channa & Rajvir S Cheema
Solo in Teental / 14th April 2008

Dr. Jyotsna Shrikanth
Carnatic Violin / 15th April 2007

07

A Near Death Experience

Author Simon Broughton

Simon Broughton
Author

Ask a man in the street in Britain to name an Indian musician and you'll get one answer, Ravi Shankar. Ask someone a little more acquainted with Indian classical instrumentalists and, after Ravi Shankar they might proffer Ali Akbar Khan, Vilayat Khan, Bismillah Khan, perhaps Amjad Ali Khan, Hariprasad Chaurasia and Shivkumar Sharma. After these, many people, certainly Westerners, will start to slow down. What's worrying is that the youngest of these musicians, sarod-player Amjad Ali Khan, is 62. The others are ten or twenty years older and two of them are dead. If this handful of names really is the cream of Hindustani classical music, then in twenty years it will all be over. What's the customary raga for laments, because we'll need it to lament the passing of an age? Is this the end of one of mankind's most sublime achievements, an artistic culture that goes back centuries?

I exaggerate, of course. There are younger artists following in the footsteps of these masters, and many of them are their offspring and protégés. We have Anoushka Shankar, Shujaat Khan (son of Vilayat), Amaan Ali Bangash and Ayaan Ali Bangash (sons of Amjad Ali Khan), Rakesh Chaurasia (nephew of Hariprasad) and Rahul Sharma, clearly showing the importance of family lineage in Indian classical music. Yet most of these players are still sharing the concert platform with their fathers, mainly because concert promoters, particularly in the West, are afraid to go beyond the names that everybody knows. "They really were maestros," says Jay Visva Deva, who's been promoting South Asian concerts in Britain for thirty years. "And the era of this music is passing. What's missing is the soul. Today's musicians may be technically better, but the soul and the art has gone."

Of course, the respect shown towards age in South Asian culture is commendable and everyone acknowledges that breakthrough generation that brought Indian classical music to the West. But frankly, if I were a young sitar-player I'd feel like saying: shut up, give me a chance. And those new generation names listed above have actually had it easy because they can follow in the footsteps of their deified dads. "Many feel it's unfair that I've had help," says Anoushka Shankar, "not just because Ravi-ji is famous, but because in the family I was able to be personally tutored from very young." Anoushka, still in her mid-20s, started learning the sitar when she was eight and made her recording debut aged thirteen.

So how does it feel if you're not lucky enough to be born with a big name? Two of the best sitarists playing today are Shahid Parvez, aged 57, (and actually from a rather illustrious musical family) and Purbayan Chatterjee, aged 31. "People have always been obsessed with brand-value over quality," says Chatterjee phlegmatically. "This is why we pay more for branded tee-shirts or watches which may be of the same quality or inferior to generic ones. Although this is an initial disadvantage to younger musicians, I think it also helps us in trying harder every day to achieve this brand-value. However when I see musicians being discriminated against on the basis of people's notions about religion or up-bringing or family background it pains me greatly as I myself am not a star performer's son. I have had to face times in my life where people have openly expressed doubts about booking me for a concert because they prefer to go for a known name. I don't blame them for this, but see it as a personal triumph when the same organiser comes back to me a few years down the line." One of the smart moves Chatterjee also made was to do something new with the sitar. He recorded 'Samwad', a jugalbandi (duet) recording with Kala Ramnath on violin, a combination rarely, if ever, done before. Not earth-shattering, but innovative and it certainly made me take notice of a sitar-player I'd never heard of.

"Rigorous training was the old way. It did give a lot of depth and a technical advantage, but you also lost a lot of things by cutting yourself off from reality. But now things have changed and I have come to understand that that sort of training is not necessary. What's most important is a real urge on behalf of the student and to have the talent and fire within you. **Pandit Ravi Shankar**

Soumik Datta [sarod]
Sarod player / 2nd March 2006

Another idea that's become commonplace is that Indian classical music actually needs age and maturity. The musical and emotional depth in the performance requires long training, wisdom and experience. I'm not saying that the veterans have encouraged this idea, but it's certainly suited them well. But let's not forget that Ravi Shankar was in his thirties

(Purbayan Chatterjee's age) when he astonished the West with his solo recitals and far younger than Shahid Parvez when he played alongside Jimi Hendrix and Janis Joplin at Woodstock.

Ah, but what about the training? That vigorous sadhana regime of guru and disciple? Years of sleepless nights and bloody fingers worn to the bone from hours of practising. From the age of 18, Ravi Shankar spent over six years living close to his guru Allauddin Khan. He found this particularly hard as he'd spent years living a luxurious, cosmopolitan life with his brother's troupe in Paris. "I used to get up very early in the morning, practise for a few hours, then have a little breakfast, then bathe and go to him for three or four hours training," Shankar recalls. "I'd rest a little and then I'd practise all afternoon, so I was doing about 14 hours a day. But it took me six months to get into that groove and then there were flies, mosquitoes, scorpions, snakes...." How can the younger players compete with that? Without that sort of application, discipline and spiritual development, surely today's music must be shallow in comparison. "It's less forceful," says Viram Jasani of Asian Music Circuit (AMC). "There's a general trend towards technique and speed, rather than developing your ideas and aesthetic. The spirit isn't there that you found in the golden age of Indian music. There's nobody today that can match them."

Purbayan Chatterjee isn't so sure: "Over the years, generations of listeners have been fed on heavy doses of this 'spirituality' aspect, that the image of an Indian classical musician has become that of a grey-haired person who is totally detached from the real world. While it's true that Indian music is a very abstract subject and the depth of its understanding does require years of immersion, it is also true that it is a highly scientific and technical subject, the performance of which requires a great degree of physical skill. By common logic any individual is likely to be at their physical best in their 30s and 40s and this is easily proved by listening to the sheer virtuosity of the great masters in their younger days when they actually took the world by storm." Interestingly enough, Ravi Shankar absolutely concurs: "That rigorous training was the old way. It did give a lot of depth and a technical advantage, but you also lost a lot of things by cutting yourself off from reality. I was lucky because at a young age I'd already had a lot of experience of the world. But now things have changed and I have come to understand that that sort of training is not necessary. What's most important is a real urge on behalf of the student and to have the talent and fire within you."

It's not like the younger generation are just grabbing a DVD of 'How to Play Sitar in 5 Easy Lessons' and then posting a few ragas on YouTube. Kala Ramnath has outlined how she prepared herself for her career as a musician. "As a child, I did not have a normal childhood," she explains. "I never played sports lest I hurt myself and be unable to practise as a result of that. I never went out to watch movies or school picnics and study tours as that again was a form of distraction. It's the fruits of such sacrifices that the artist reaps later on in life." So there is a philosophical dimension, at least, to this sort of training. You have to make sacrifices, but hopefully you reap rewards.

There's also the problem that many of the best musicians live abroad or are travelling a lot. So who is training the new generation? "And today's gurus don't have the time to teach and musicians don't have the patience to learn," adds Jay Visva Deva. "Today's world moves much faster. Even in India audiences for classical music are dwindling because their attention-span is limited. India is rushing and has woken up after 60 years." But maybe music should change with the

Harmeet Virdee [sitar]
Raag Mian Ki Todi / 3rd March 2006

times – shouldn't it reflect the world we live in? Does a style of music created for refined audiences in the royal courts of the Moghuls have any place in democratic India with its economy booming on IT and mobile phones?

Of course, an artist like Purbayan Chatterjee, who has a sideline in devising raga ringtones, still sees a place for classical music, but suggests a two-pronged approach to making a career: "First, a chiselling of one's art to be able to rise above any criticism and then a strategically defined marketing of one's abilities. Before you bleed your fingers to death practising, think again – you may need them to type that email which gets you your biggest break."

Record companies have been slow to record them, promoters have been slow to programme them and audiences have been slow to try them. Sense World Music have been good at recording the younger generations of musicians – perhaps because as relative newcomers they haven't had long-established relationships with the older generation. Asian Music Circuit promote many concerts and education projects in the UK each year. Similarly, the Darbar team should be commended for programming younger artists in the Darbar Festival. Both AMC and Darbar receive Arts Council support, so it's scary to think what the situation would be like without that.

Journalists and writers are also to blame. So often what you read about a musician is little more than who his or her father was or who they studied with. This is just lazy. Writers, particularly in India, need to start writing more creatively and more insightfully about the music. It's not easy to do, but if artists, promoters and journalists apply themselves to the next generation then audiences can discover that the Hindustani music tradition, a sublime fusion of Hindu and Muslim ingredients that started melding in the Moghul Empire from the 16th century, continues as a living and developing form today.

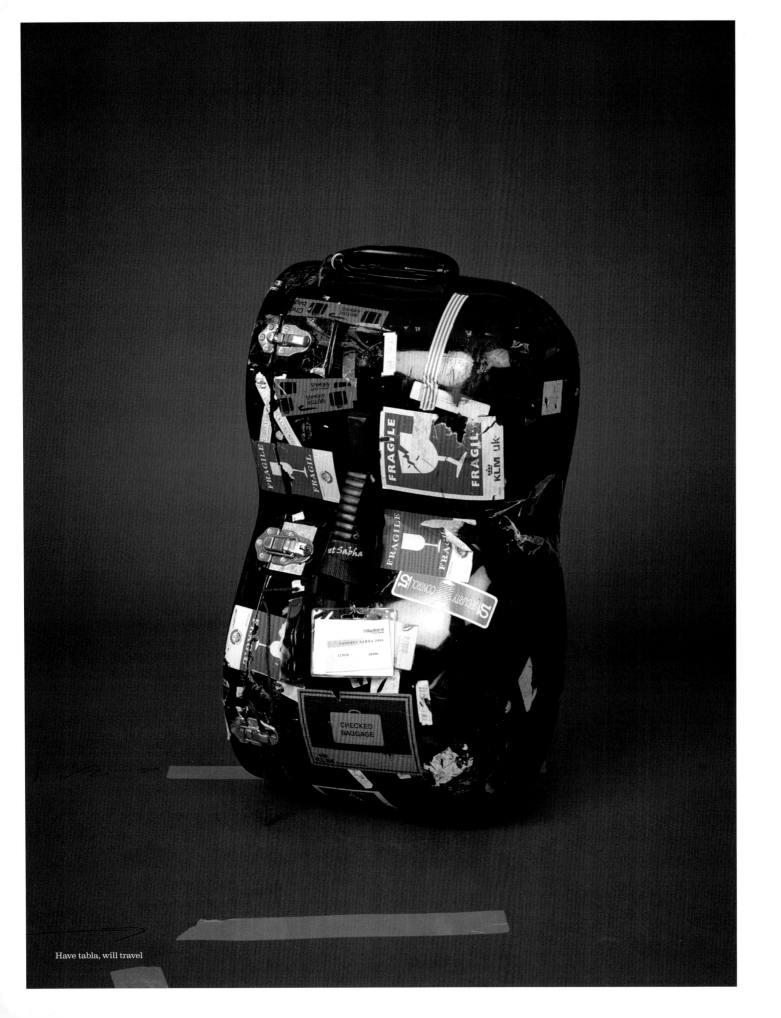

Have tabla, will travel

So often what you read about a musician is little more than who his or her father was or who they studied with. This is just lazy. Writers, particularly in India, need to start writing more creatively and more insightfully about the music. **Simon Broughton**

08
Classical Music, Contemporary Attitude

Author James Burkmar

James Burkmar
Author

I think I have lost count now of the number of times I have found myself in a discussion on the difference between art and heritage. If you then add in the question "what do we mean by culture" then it's pretty fair to say that the discussion will become more heated and more confused. Clearly for some it's a hot topic, one that needs defining. For others it's a small point really, something that occupies very little time or headspace. Let me be clear, I expect to offer no clarity here, maybe though a question or two more.

Where people do tend to agree is that all of these things tell us something about ourselves. How we chose or choose to spend our time. How we have expressed ourselves, how we have tried to make sense of life, love, emotions and the rest. There have even been times in history when these things have been revered, celebrated, hidden away, denied or even burned. Clearly then there is something going on here that reaches us, defines us, maybe even helps us makes sense of who we are and possibly helps us make sense of the lives we lead.

For a few years I worked for Arts Council England, a place where these questions came up with alarming frequency. Our role was to provide funding support for the arts so defining art as opposed to heritage became a pretty critical question. Once in a while along came someone, or something that made life even more confusing. That's how I met Darbar.

Across a period of three to four months I met up with Sandeep, Derek, Alpesh and Ashok, all of whom were engaged in this idea known as Darbar. I knew of them through their respective enterprises. Tablaonline whose committed, entrepreneurial approach had impressed immediately. Sense World Music with their uncompromising intent to record and reveal to the world beautiful acoustic Indian classical music. And there the confusion began with this world we call classical. Whatever your dictionary says, the word feels like it's there to describe something that's defined already, something that stood the test of time, something you revere for its self-evident value, something that does not invite you to do anything other than acknowledge its universally agreed specialness, like Shakespeare or Mars bars.

When Darbar eventually manifested at Leicester's Peepul Centre in 2006 it was to honour the late Bhai Gurmit Singh Virdee. Darbar drew musicians from across the oceans, apparently effortlessly, with the desire in their heart to pay respects and honour the passing of a great man and musician, and to play some music.

With a sense of expectation and yet unsure of what to expect I attended the festival three times in its long weekend. On one occasion I attended with my seven-year-old daughter. We wandered around, listened, watched, and experienced all manner of things. Great concerts with electrifying performances from musicians who appeared possessed in their desire to breathe life into the moment through blistering playing and technique; elders and musicians holding court spontaneously with gaggles of engaged concert-goers forming some kind of well-dressed roadblock around the venue's corridors and spaces; workshops led by musicians closer to my daughter's age than mine, with an exuberance and informality that disarmed all who attended; musical instruments being wielded like deadly weapons yet with the appearance of delicately carved works of art which would crumble at the merest breath.

The word classical, the word heritage, both of which I have myself attributed so often to this musical form were evaporating from my arts council lexicon like so much hot air.

How could this be? Through music events and conferences I had met some of the people here today in decidedly more sedate moments and settings. Was this then what Darbar was really about?

Classical feels like it's there to describe something that's defined already, something that stood the test of time, something you revere for its self-evident value, something that does not invite you to do anything other than acknowledge its universally agreed specialness, like Shakespeare or Mars bars.
James Burkmar

Pandit Tejendra Majumdar, Mysore Manjunath and Arjun Kumar
Raag Charukesi / 4th March 2006

Darbar with its commitment and links to the Saptak festival in the Indian state of Gujarat. Darbar with a desire so strong to profile the music and musicians integral to this form that it built its own recording studio close to the festival. Darbar with its living, breathing ambitions drawn up in plans, charts and documents which if ever given the chance would redefine the Indian classical music industry in this country. Darbar with its passion for new artists from the UK, its relationships with some of the greatest musicians of the age, its leadership and desire to suggest collaborations that renew and refresh the very thing that they love.

This kind of energy, this kind of spark, this kind of essence is hard to come by. Heritage, the arts, culture, they all melt away at moments like this. As I write Darbar is building new partnerships for the future with venues, funders, musicians, audiences and museums and if half of what they discuss is achieved we shall all bear witness to a redefining of terms, which should give funders a few more problems in years to come, bringing this living heritage to new audiences, places and spaces.

And that's the word for me, living. When I asked my daughter at the festival that time what she thought the word classical meant she answered excitedly "...something special and old... but I think it might be dead ...". From the mouths of babes.

Shahswati Mandal Paul [tappa vocal]
Raag Sohini / 6th April 2008

Pandit Vishwa Mohan Bhatt and Pandit Yogesh Samsi
Raag Kaunsi Kanra / 14th April 2007

Shahbaz Hussain on tabla and Rajen Mistry
Clearing flour from previous night's concert!

Smt Kaushiki Chakraborty, Sandeep Virdee, Ranjana Ghatak and Dr Debipriya Das
Sound checks / 5th April 2008

Bhupinder S Chaggar [tabla]
Solo in Teental / 5th April 2008

Gunwant Kaur and Bhupinder S Chaggar
A standing ovation for UK talent

Pandit Nayan Ghosh
Sound Checks / 6th April 2008

Pandit Nayan Ghosh with Pandit Sanju Sahai
Raag Mian Ki Todi / 6th April 2008

Tarun Jasani [sarod]
Raag Jaunpuri / 4th April 2008

09

Great Traditions in Little Villages

Author **Rolf Killius**

Rolf Killius
Author

Most people in Britain are aware that there is more to Indian culture than Shilpa Shetty, the Bollywood actress, who received fame from the reality television show, Big Brother. Many may also be aware that aside from the north Indian classical Hindustani tradition of music and the carnatic tradition from the south, there is so much more. During several extended visits to India, I came across an extraordinary variety of elaborate music styles in every nook and corner of India, styles that are relatively unheard of in India let alone the West.

In 2008, London's Horniman Museum opened a temporary exhibition focused on many of these rural musical traditions. The exhibition, Utsavam – Music from India (Utsavam means celebration or festival in Sanskrit) presents more than 300 musical instruments and around 40 short films, mostly brought together during extensive fieldwork trips over several years.

Curated by Margaret Birley, the Horniman's Keeper of Musical Instruments and the ethnomusicologist Rolf Killius, the exhibition displays musical instruments, photographs, sound and video recordings of music and people from several parts of India. Arranged in five sections, it emphasises the village-dwelling majority of India's population, including the Adivasi (indigenous) groups whose music remains relatively unknown. The artists and musical instrument makers whose work is presented represent the four main language groups of India (Dravidian, Indo-Aryan, Tibeto-Burman and Austroasiatic). The exhibition also features a Punjabi sarangi (bowed string instrument) and Assamese drum makers' workshops.

It brings together the music and dance traditions of the temple musicians in rural Kerala, musician-farmers of the villages of the Sora (Adivasi of Orissa and Andhra Pradesh), singer-storytellers from Punjab, fishermen and farmers on the river island of Majuli in Assam, and musicians of the Buddhist Monpa community in the Eastern Himalayas of Arunachal Pradesh just below the Chinese/Tibetan border. Videos of festivals, rituals, instrument-making and performances in their own environments can be seen on video screens and on a small cinema set. The stories are told by musicians, community elders and instruments' makers themselves.

The Horniman also displays instruments from its renowned permanent collection focusing on the rural and the two classical traditions. Some were collected by the Museum founder, Frederick Horniman, a tea merchant and philanthropist who travelled to India in 1894 and 1896.

The story of the exhibition goes back to the year 2000 when Janet Topp Fargion, the curator of the World and Traditional Music Section in the British Library Sound Archive, and Rolf Killius, set up a research project to record, document and research India's folk, devotional and ritual music. Part of the project became the collection and documentation of more than 100 musical instruments for the Horniman Museum. Subsequently, the Museum commissioned musical instruments to be made in the areas, where the music and dance was recorded.

Between 2002 and 2007, Rolf Killius, camera-woman Jutta Winkler, and Margaret Birley went to Kerala, Orissa, Andhra Pradesh, Assam, Arunachal Pradesh and Punjab to spend some three years researching, collecting and documenting material for the exhibition. Repeated visits established close relationships with the musicians and instrument makers and ensured direct input and feedback from them. Within the Sora communities in Orissa, the work for the exhibition in London instigated the wish to establish a Sora Adivasi Museum and Cultural Centre in their own area.

" This landmark exhibition (Utsavam — Music from India) at the Horniman, and the programme of events around it, offer a new perspective on Indian culture and music. I am sure it will inspire people to discover more about Indian music and provide artistic influence to musicians here in the UK.
Nitin Sawhney, musician and exhibition patron "

well-documented, little work has been done on more remote rural areas and the Adivasi people who comprise around 7% of the total population. In many areas music and dance cultures could be regarded as 'endangered' because of the rapidly changing socio-economic fabric and the traditionally high stratification in Indian society. So far, India's superfast highway of 'modernisation' has had little benefit for the majority of rural and Adivasi people. Traditional music is largely being marginalised through the prevalence of Hindi pop music. And traditional musicians are forced to leave their long-established occupations with the hope of employment in the towns and cities.

Some researchers, enthusiasts, and music promoters have started to highlight the varied rural, regional, and Adivasi music genres still prevalent all over India. They emphasise the aesthetic beauty of the music and dances. But researchers are beginning to come round to the opinion that these mainly oral art forms need to be considered as intangible historical, socio-religious, and musicological traditions that belong to the world's cultural heritage, and need to be treated in the same way as books and manuscripts kept in libraries. For instance, the South Indian Toda people preserve their history in chants; and the minstrels of the Chakmas communities in north-east India and Bangladesh remember their historical wandering routes through ballads performed by bards.

Many regional and local music styles are related and influenced by the classical tradition but one could debate the rather rigid divisions of 'margi-desi sangeet' or 'great and little traditions', where 'great' stands for 'classical' and little for 'local' or 'folk' music genres. Criteria for the 'great traditions' like professional status and systematic training of the musicians could be applied to many of the so-called 'little traditions'. In general, Indian music genres consist of complex and interrelated traditions, established on a secular-sacred, more-or-less canonised continuum; and performed by professional, semi-professional and amateur musicians.

Focusing on the oral culture of distinct communities living in some of the more remote rural areas, where music and dance still play an important part in everyday life, the exhibition is the first major step to make the collected musical instruments and some of the sound and film material from these areas available to the public.

The exhibition also extends beyond the glass cabinets. Community, cultural and heritage organisation provided a 'live', participatory element. Highlights included the Raj Academy Ensemble presenting traditions passed down by the Sikh Gurus, the Tamil temple singer Sami Dhandapani, the London Sitar Ensemble, the Sutton Subrang Dance Ensemble, Samay – London meets India, and Somjit Dasgupta from Kolkata. Darbar presented a series of music recitals, including a day of performances from the two classical traditions from both North and South India. Dance performances included the renowned Kathakali dancer Kalamandalam Vijayakumar, Mohiniyattam by Parvati Nair, Assamese Sattria dance by Rupali Barooah, Odissi by Katharine Ryan and Kathak by Crishna Budhu. During the summer, a colourful Mela attracted thousands of people to the beautiful Horniman gardens.

School children have been actively involved. A six-month project led by the Asian Dub Foundation Education and students from The Archbishop Lanfranc School in Croydon created live percussion pieces mixed with electronic and fieldwork audio tracks, which they performed live at the exhibition's opening.

To coincide with the opening the British Forum for Ethnomusicology and Horniman Museum jointly organised a nationwide conference at the Museum entitled Soundscapes of India: Tradition, Transformation and Topography, where scholars and students involved in Indian music debated modern trends in traditional Indian music.

The Utsavam – Music from India exhibition is more than just music and dance. It is about the people, who play, sing, and listen and dance. Music and dance is one important part of a rich identity, that links them to their tradition and understand the real world.

In the West, there is a new awareness of Indian music and this is being helped by the world wide web as it connects rural musicians with people throughout the world to create new possibilities to continue and revive their age-old trade. The exhibition producers fear that due to the rapid socio-economic changes in India some of the music styles and ritual practices shown in the exhibition could disappear forever. But they also hope that some of the rural musicians and instrument makers can be encouraged to continue and develop their profession and find a wider audience. It is not just about recording and documenting, but also about exchanging ideas and understanding to create awareness of these artists and culture, and link them to other musicians in India and elsewhere.

After I introduced the Horniman exhibition to the last annual conference of the Indian Musicological Society in Mumbai one student asked me what use it is to 'show ritual music of India to a western audience?' The answer should possibly be, that traditional Indian music, as any traditional music in the world, has foremost an aesthetic value, can be appreciated by everyone to whom it is introduced, and therefore must be regarded as part of the world's cultural heritage. The Horniman Museum's exhibition Utsavam – Music from India is a step in this direction.

"Researchers are beginning to come round to the opinion that these mainly oral art forms need to be considered as intangible historical, socio-religious, and musicological traditions that belong to the world's cultural heritage, and need to be treated in the same way as books and manuscripts kept in libraries. **Rolf Killius**

Photo of Sat Guru Jagjit Singh
spiritual successor of Naamdhari Sikhs

Bhai Surjeet Singh [sarangi] with Surdarshan Singh [jori]
Darbar Festival at the Horniman Museum, London / 30th March 2008

Darbar Festival at the V&A, London Ustad Irshad Khan [sitar] and Shahbaz Hussain [tabla]
Raag Patdeep / 13th April 2008

Ken Zuckerman [sarod]

Ken Zuckerman, Pandit Yogesh Samsi and Pandit Ravi Shankar Upaday
Darbar 'unplugged' concert at Richard Attenborough Centre, Leicester / 11th April 2007

10
Sculpting With Air

Author Derek Roberts

"Recording music is one of the most important ways of developing and preserving cultural heritage. It is amazing how methods and approaches to music can be lost within one or two generations, so it is important to foster the arts through recorded work.
Derek Roberts

Derek Roberts
Author

'Chai, chai garam chai, sandwich, wada wada, cutlet cutlet, limbo pani, tunda limbo pani' the food sellers chanted in their unique and distinctive way as the train slowly made its way from Mumbai to Ahmedabad, Gujarat. As the wheels continued their ever-changing rhythmic patterns over the tracks, I sat and marvelled at the colourful craziness of India and delighted to smell new smells and hear new sounds, sounds which now feel as familiar as if I had heard them for many lifetimes. I had arrived in India.

In the last eight years or so many of you may know me through my work with Sense World Music, a record label specialising in Indian classical music. The agenda at Sense has been to develop a record company which has deep creative consideration and consistently high quality of production to enable listeners to appreciate more fully the potential beauty of Indian classical music through releases of CDs and DVDs. Many of the label's releases have won rave reviews and plaudits across the globe and have helped great new talents to flourish and develop their profiles which in turn gives musicians the opportunity to earn a living from international touring and related work.

Recording music is one of the most important ways of developing and preserving cultural heritage. It is amazing how methods and approaches to music can be lost within one or two generations, so it is important to foster the arts through recorded work. Recording also provides artists with a valuable marker as to where they are in their development and a chance to reflect and make progress. The quality of the recording is essential to this process.

The legendary rock guitarist and composer Frank Zappa once coined a phrase that composing and improvising is really 'sculpting with air'.

Many years ago, inspired by thoughts of the interconnectedness of things, I began to explore more deeply the relationship between how music is motivated from within the mind of the musician and how sound is generated from an instrument or the human body. I then thought about how this interacts with air, environment, sound equipment, sensory perception and the mind of the listener. Understanding these different facets of the creative process and sound production is now the basis of much of my work these days as a producer and sound engineer. I, like the performing musician, am also 'sculpting with air'.

Musicians and sound engineers have a relationship. We are both manipulating and transmitting sound as a way of communicating intentions, emotions and artistic values. The quality of this transmission is important if we are going to appreciate the music being generated.

How is an appropriate level of quality achieved? By the development of well-rounded artists from beginners into advanced musicians, by developing excellence of sound production in both live and recorded situations and by developing appreciative listeners with hopefully good quality hi-fi! Of course there are also so many technical aspects to sound production which cannot be explained now, that is for a different book.

We can use a simple analogy here. Imagine there is a beautiful scene outside the window but the window is dirty. The truth is that you will not fully appreciate the scene until the barrier of dirt which hinders your view is removed. You are sometimes surprised how nice it is when you have clean windows, right? It is like this with sound production. Bad quality sound obscures 'our view' of the music and hinders our potential appreciation and enjoyment. It is something which has dogged Indian music for decades where things have historically been done on the cheap with little consideration for the music. This has happened for lots of reasons, but there are a couple which are particularly relevant; one is lack of finance

is a minority art form, and another is lack of understanding and education on behalf of musicians and engineers.

Another thing which can add a particular quality to music is the intention of the musician. This is a more subtle point to understand. If a musician has a positive motivation and a mind which is 'centred', the depth of feeling within them will be much stronger and this can be projected through the music. So making music is not just an external process of producing sound, it is an inner process, a process of the mind.

South Asian musical heritage is steeped in spiritual and philosophical tradition and it is this more ancient influence, which still flows through the music today. However, if the inner process of music-making is lost then the ancient spiritual heritage of the music will also be lost. It should be mentioned here that this inner process is not limited to one cultural tradition, since the spiritual creative process itself knows no boundaries and discriminations set up by human beings. Wherever there is a musician who has a depth of spirituality, there is a chance for this to come through in the music. We can be trained to do this with the correct methods. It is therefore important for musicians to nurture this side of their development.

'Sculpting with air' could be defined as 'the manipulation of air using vibrational energy by a creative person such as a musician or sound engineer in order to communicate.'

Through intense years of working with Indian music a number of things become very clear. The above definition has deep significance for Indian classical music and any other musical form which has improvisation at its heart, because spontaneous creativity allows us to communicate 'in the moment' with others and it has a vibrant life full of surprises.

Improvisation creates the potentiality for the music to touch the deepest aspect of our mind or our 'soul' and also produces really exciting performance which can transport us to a 'different place' as long as a musician has the technical capacity, the right intentions of mind and is 'in the zone' when he or she is playing. The listener also has to be in the right 'zone' to tune in to this. When the process works well, we feel deeply the emotions relating to the piece being played and we can almost feel the mind of the musician as he is creating. It can be quite a transcendent spiritual experience!

This way of creating and listening is of even more relevance if you consider the deeper spiritual influences and origins within the music. The right conditions, however, have to come together for music-making of this type and for sound to occur at all!

Let's look at a philosophical angle on music-making and sound production to find out why.

Quite simply, without all the necessary causes and conditions for music to occur it does not appear at all if you take out one of the different elements of the process. For instance, if there is no mind of the musician there is no music. If there is no instrument or voice there is no music. If there is no air, there is no music. If there is no apprehending consciousness i.e. the mind(s) of the musician or audience there is no music. Music like all phenomena that we perceive is therefore a dependent relationship of lots of different things; it does not exist as an independent phenomena and ultimately depends upon the mind and is not separate from it. Each element is therefore very important.

Ok, so now you probably realise there is a potential connection between spirituality, sound and music, and the music of India in particular, not least because the deepest spiritual philosophical tenets have been expounded in India since ancient times. The above explanation of how music appears was taught by Buddha in his wisdom teachings on the ultimate nature of phenomena, the teachings that explain the true nature of reality and how all things exist. He also taught that all things including our self are merely appearances to mind and that cherishing our self above the welfare of others is the root of all suffering. It is our grasping at a self we feel is

Pandit Purbayan Chatterjee [sitar]
Raag Jog Kauns / 6th April 2008

Pandit Bickram Ghosh, Pete Locket,
Jesse Bannister, Mounir Baziz and Guliano Modarelli
SUNEV / 5th April 2008

Shahbaz Hussain
Tabla / 19th April 2008

"Imagine there is a beautiful scene outside the window but the window is dirty. The truth is that you will not fully appreciate the scene until the barrier of dirt which hinders your view is removed. It is like this with sound production. Bad quality sound obscures 'our view' of the music and hinders our potential appreciation and enjoyment.
Derek Roberts

solid and 'really there' that gets in the way of so much in life, including our creative activities.

Creative activity can provide an opportunity for us to let go of our self and become a channel for positive spiritual energy. This method of creating gets rid of the conceptualising that can sometimes hinder this special creative flow. If we have a positive motivation towards others, wishing them happiness and freedom from suffering, our mind becomes peaceful and stable. While we maintain this mind we let go of our self because we think of others instead of our self. If we create in this way, our self is kept out of the process and we are sometimes able to channel higher spiritual energy, which manifests in the form and medium we are creating with whether it be movement, paint, sand or vibrations passing through air in the form of music. If we can learn to maintain this 'open state', it is as though our mind has been blessed by higher consciousness and we channel this energy into the creative process. The quality of this process depends as with everything, upon the mind.

If we were to develop our wisdom and depth of spirituality along with rigorous practise of music, oh how there would be the potential for sublime music!

So what of the future of South Asian music? Any minority art form needs support and all of us on a personal level can help. There is always great talent out there that can be nurtured. It would be great to see more bursaries and funds available to help individual musicians go through a clear artist development programme. We need a music industry that can survive and we need the right concert platforms available. We need great marketing and professionalism in all aspects of the work. We all need to work together.

This is a time when the music business is in crisis with mass and personal piracy at crazy proportions, due in the main to the ease of use of new technology and a common public mentality which is 'if I can get it for free I will'.

So everyone go to the concerts and buy the music! Don't destroy the thing you love by copying it and denying the funds needed to keep musicians, record company and the whole thing going.

In valuing cultural heritage we become connected to others around us in a positive way and we tap into the creative power of those who have gone before us. It is forces such as these which can give our lives a greater meaning.

So, if you fancy experiencing a clearer view of Indian classical music, sit back and relax in front of a state-of-the-art hi-fi in a good listening room, after an ear-syringe and a hearing test. Then with a clear, open and patient mind (preferably after a short breathing meditation) take a listen to perhaps Desert Slide with Vishwa Mohan Bhatt and the great musicians of Rajasthan; the groups called Chakra, Yashila or Mandala; or the CD Talaash from Purbayan Chatterjee and you will understand!

Hary Kumar Siva
[7 string electric violin]
Raag / 14th April 2008

11
The Future of Technology in North Indian Music

Author Dharambir Singh Dhadyalla

The spirit of the time is making many individuals think on how to use the available technology for the enjoyment, learning and preservation of Indian music. The tide is too strong and the future bright where knowledge would be available in various formats for the students and the listeners with far more ease than has been in the past.
Dharambir Singh Dhadyalla

Dharambir Singh Dhadyalla
Author

Throughout history human beings have expressed themselves musically in a variety of ways. The evolution of musical instruments is a good example of the technologies in action. The relatively recent advent of the computer is opening up amazing opportunities as a tool for making music. It is quite evident that the western world has taken a lead in using the synthesised sounds. Indian musicians involved in the classical music have not been very impressed by the digital sound available through the synthesizers. The main reason for this could be that it has mainly come from the western tuning systems of the equal temperament. The equal temperament though a great convenience, has not, however, appealed to the Indian musician, as it is far removed from the natural sounds or the natural overtones. But new technologies are around the corner and they will make the production of the natural intonations or tones of the harmonic series much more accessible.

The use of technology will surely impact the appreciation of Indian music, live music, recordings and the learning of music. The importance of visualisation of music is well established in Indian music. The Ragmala paintings are an example of the efforts of giving Ragas a visual meaning. The hand gestures of the singers are another example of making music visual. The tali (clap, count and wave) of the various tals is another use of the visual cues in musical time keeping. So what is the future technology and Indian music?

More and more use of the colour and shape visualisation, special to the rags and the talas will become common both in the appreciation and the learning of Indian music. The various moods of the ragas will not only be felt but seen through colours. The listener would not only be fed through the ears but also the eyes. Various projects have realised this approach in accompanying visuals to Western music. Experiments have been done by some composers in creating visuals accompanying Indian ragas. However, there is no software available which allows musicians to programme it to what they see in ragas. Such software would add another dimension where each tone of the Indian gamut can be assigned a colour and its use in a live performance would generate a collage of colours true to the raga created by the musician. It would also be a tool to compare the same ragas sung or played by different artists. This kind of a tool could also help trigger the creativity of the musician in producing music in interaction with computer software.

Voice-training software is also becoming popular. There are a number of programmes available for the students of Western music. Computer programmes that would allow the students of Indian music to see the melodic lines visually as curves would be very welcome. These melodic lines, like graphs, would allow students to reproduce the smooth curves special to this music. These applications would also be very useful for the researchers in analysing the various bandishes (song compositions) in gleaning the information of the ragas, seeing the key phrases of the ragas and playing around with these.

The visualisation of the intricate rhythm work within Indian music is another important area which will be looked at by various interested people. It will be helpful to the listeners and the students to be able to interact with computer software in order to hear their rhythmic ideas being played back. The use of numbers in Indian music is very important. The creation of tihayis (rhythmic cadences) and the complex layakari (complex rhythmic interplay) could be enhanced by the availability of special softwares.

Most Indian instruments need a musician with a good ear for tuning. A sitarist, sarod player or sarangi player can tell you how important the art of tuning their sympathetic strings to the tones of the ragas is. The whole resonance of the raga cannot be created without the internal harmonic balance in the tones.

Traditionally the students of Indian music pick up the tunings by listening to their teachers or their peers. The capacity of the student to digest these tunings depends on their inherent musical aptitude. Some do find it very hard and could take many years before they are comfortable in tuning an instrument independently. Some even resort to the chromatic tuners available for the Western music market. These chromatic tuners do not have the capacity to generate tones demanded by Indian music. A small gadget in the form of a tuner giving the main twelve tones of just intonation, (which would be more appropriate for Indian music), with further finer tunings to generate the tones prevalent in the modern day raga performances will be a great help to the musician.

The software palette by Justonic of Canada is able to tune the synthesizers on the fly in real time. This should appeal to the Indian musicians and in particular the students to play the keyboards assigned to the tunings appropriate to the ragas. This would be a great aid for the beginners who cannot otherwise differentiate between the tones to train their ears before they approach advanced music teachers.

The last ten years have seen a rapid advancement in the various electronic machines available in the market. The tanpura machines made by Radel and Ragini now use the real digital samples of the tanpuras. They are much more stable and useful. Tabla machines have improved with programmable features and so have the nagma or lehra machines for percussionists. Even traditionalists use these machines. In my visit to the USA, I was amazed to see my Guru, Ustad Vilayat Khan, in love with his tanpura and tabla machines. He was really excited by these and saw the future bright for Indian music student.

Some free softwares are also becoming available with facilities for the musicians to select tanpuras, metronomes and tabla thekas (rhythmic drum patterns) as loops. Some specialist sequencers for Indian music are in the market with a selection of VST instruments. Notation softwares special to Indian music have been developed and are in use. A modern student of Indian music has a lot on offer to help practice in order to enhance the musicianship.

The zeitgeist (spirit of the time) is definitely making

many individuals think on how to use the available technology for the enjoyment, learning and preservation of Indian music. The tide is too strong and the future bright where knowledge would be available in various formats for the students and the listeners with far more ease than has been in the past. It is likely to be a future with an explosion of DVDs and the internet content for teaching Indian music that build on the modest offering of online teaching that is currently available. As for the future of Gurukulas (traditional music schools), well, I'll leave readers to speculate on how they may shape up.

Shahswati Mandal Paul
An interview with a BBC reporter
4th April 2008

Prafull Shah, Advisor to Saptak Festival, India

Pandit Subhankar Bannerjee
Tabla / 3rd March 2006

Pandit Ravi Shankar Upadhay
on Pakhawaj / 4th March 2006

Darbar 'unplugged'
The Guild Hall, Leicester / 2nd March 2006

In conversation with Ustad Bahauddin Dagar
5th March 2006

Sound engineer, Derek Roberts looking on

Kaviraj and Upneet Singh Dhadyalla
An interview for Sky Arts / 6th April 2008

Arjun Kumar [mridangam]
4th March 2006

Pandit Subhankar Bannerjee with Pandit Swapan Chaudhuri
Moments before Swapan Ji closes the first Darbar Festival / 5th March 2006

Musicians and organisers
after the Darbar Festival 2006

Musicians and Shivir students
Darbar Festival 2007

Gurmit Singh Virdee with his wife
and companion Mohinder Kaur
Virdee at the school in Kenya where
he taught in the 1960s.

(Mohinder Singh — :—) گت پرن (:— 2nd MARCH, 196

Ustad Bahadur Singh

دھٹ دھٹ کڑ دھا تٹ کڑ دھان نگ تٹ . تگ ۔ دھیں گن نن
تک دھر دھر کٹ تک ت کٹ دھا | کٹ تک : تک دھر دھر کٹ تک تد ت کٹ
دھا | کٹ تک تک : تک دھر دھر کٹ تک تک ت کٹ ت | دھا

tad B. Sunder Singh. — :— چلہ دار پرن :— تہریلی

دھر دھر کٹ تک تک ت کٹ دھا، دھر دھر کٹ تک تک ت کٹ دھا، دھر دھر کٹ
تک ت کٹ دھا ۔ ت کٹ دھا ت کٹ دھا ۔ دھر دھر کٹ تک تک
دھر دھر کٹ تک تک تک دھر دھر کٹ تک تک تک دھر دھر کٹ تک ت کٹ دھا
نگ دھے ن دھا گدی گن دھا، نگ دھے ن دھا گدی گن دھا
نا تا کے ک دھا، دھر دھر کٹ تک ت کٹ نا تا کے ک دھا
دھر دھر کٹ تک ت کٹ دھا نا تا کے ک دھا دھر دھر کٹ تک تک تک
دھا | اس طرے دو تین بار ۔ ۔
تک تک دھا

Ustad Bahadur Singh. — :— چلہ دار پرن :— تہریلی

Ustad Bahadur Singh, (قاعدہ تین تال) 1st Oct, 59

دھاگے نا دھا تر کٹ دھاگے دھنا کٹ تک دھر دھر کٹ تک دھر دھر کٹ
تک تاگے نا دھا تر کٹ دھاگے تنا کنا | تا گے نا تا تر کٹ دھاگے د
کٹ تک دھر دھر کٹ تک دھر دھر کٹ تک تاگے نا دھا تر کٹ دھاگے دھنا

—: پلٹے :—

(۱) دھاگے نا دھا تر کٹ دھا دھا گے نا دھا تر کٹ دھا دھا گے نا دھا تر کٹ د
دھنا کٹ تک دھر دھر کٹ تک : دھا گے نا دھا تر کٹ دھاگے دھنا کٹ تک
دھر دھر کٹ تک دھر دھر کٹ تک تاگے نا دھا تر کٹ دھاگے د
نا تا تر کٹ دھا دھا گے نا دھا تر کٹ دھا دھا گے نا دھا تر کٹ دھاگے د
کٹ تک دھر دھر کٹ تک : دھا گے نا دھا تر کٹ دھاگے دھنا کٹ تک دھر د
کٹ تک دھر دھر کٹ تک تاگے نا دھا تر کٹ نا دھا تر کٹ دھاگے دھنا کنا |

(۲) دھاگے نا دھا تر کٹ دھا .. دھا گے نا دھا تر کٹ دھاگے دھنا ک
تک دھر دھر کٹ تک دھا تر کٹ نا دھا تر کٹ : دھا گے نا دھا تر کٹ دھاگے د

Photographers Index

Arnhel de Serra

Chapter 1
P. 12 / 13 / 14 / 15 / 16 / 17 / 18 / 19 / 22 / 23 / 24 / 27 / 28 / 29 / 30 / 31

Chapter 2
P. 38 / 39 / 41 / 42 / 43 / 44 / 45 46 / 47 / 48 / 51 / 58 / 59 / 60 / 61 / 62 / 63 / 64 / 65

Chapter 3
P. 70 / 71 / 72 / 73

Chapter 4
P. 84 / 88 / 89 / 94 / 95

Chapter 5
P. 100 / 101 / 102—103 / 105 / 107 / 108 / 109 / 110—111 / 115 / 116—117 / 118—119

Chapter 6
P. 125 / 129 / 130—131 / 132 / 133 135 / 136 / 138

Chapter 7
P. 144

Chapter 8
P. 153 / 154—155 / 158 / 159 / 160 161 / 162—163 / 164 / 165

Chapter 10
P. 186 / 187 / 188 / 189

Chapter 11
P. 196 / 197 / 198 / 200—201 202—203 / 204 / 205 / 206 / 207 / 208 / 209 / 210—211

P. 62 / 68 / 72 / 79

Jonathan Worth

Chapter 1
P. 20 / 21

Chapter 2
P. 40

Chapter 4
P. 90

Chapter 5
P. 106

Chapter 6
P. 126 / 127 / 128

Chapter 7
P. 142 / 146

Chapter 8
P. 152

Chapter 11
P. 199 / 214—215 / 216—217

Sandeep Singh Virdee

Chapter 1
P. 25 / 32—33

Chapter 2
P. 52—53 / 54—55

Chapter 3
P. 74 / 76—77

Chapter 7
P. 156—157

Chapter 6
P. 126 / 127 / 128

Chapter 7
P. 142 / 146

Rajen Mistry

Chapter 2
P. 56—57

Chapter 3
P. 78 / 79

Chapter 4
P. 84 / 94—95

Chapter 5
P. 120—121

Chapter 6
P. 136 / 137

Chapter 7
P. 143

Chapter 8
P. 156—157

Chapter 9
P. 180 / 181

Chapter 10
P. 191

Rehmat Rayatt

Chapter 4
P. 87 / 93

Anjali Desai

Chapter 4
P. 85

Raju Srivastav
Sense World Music
Photographer

Chapter 4
P. 91

Gurwinder Singh Soor

P. 6

Surjeet Singh Virdee

Chapter 11
P. 212—213

Anonymous

Chapter 11
P. 218